the vegetarian cookbook

the
vegetarian
cookbook

more than **150** healthy, easy, and satisfying recipes

Reader's Digest

The Reader's Digest Association, Inc.
Pleasantville, New York • Montreal

A READER'S DIGEST BOOK

PROJECT TEAM
Editor: Lisa Thomas
Copy Editor: Jill Steed
Designer: Jane McKenna
Nutritionist: Fiona Hunter
U.S. Project Editor: Barbara Booth
U.S. Consulting Editor: Andrea Chesman
Canadian Project Editor: Pamela Chichinskas
Project Production Coordinator: Wayne Morrison
Indexer: Andrea Chesman
Cover Designer: Mabel Zorzano
Associate Art Director: George McKeon
Executive Editor, Trade Publishing: Dolores York
Production Manager: Elizabeth Dinda
Vice President and Director of Production: Michael Braunschweiger
Associate Publisher: Rosanne McManus
President and Publisher, U.S. Trade Publishing: Harold Clarke

Library of Congress Cataloging in Publication Data
The vegetarian cookbook: more than 150 healthy, easy, and satisfying recipes /
from the editors of Reader's Digest.—1st ed.
     p.cm.
     ISBN 13: 978-0-7621-0900-5 (paperback)
     ISBN 13: 978-0-7621-0924-1 (hardcover)
Vegetarian cookery. I. Reader's Digest Association.
TX837.V4235 2008
641.5'636—dc26   2007036658

We are committed to both the quality of our products and the service
we provide to our customers. We value your comments, so please feel
free to contact us.

> The Reader's Digest Association, Inc.
> Adult Trade Publishing
> Reader's Digest Road
> Pleasantville, NY 10570-7000

For more Reader's Digest products and information, visit our website:
     www.rd.com (in the United States)
     www.readersdigest.ca (in Canada)

Printed in China

1 3 5 7 9 10 8 6 4 2 (paperback)
1 3 5 7 9 10 8 6 4 2 (hardcover)

Why eat vegetarian?

In the U.S. today, 4 to 10 percent of the population consider themselves to be vegetarians, following a diet that excludes fish, meat, and any animal by-products. A smaller proportion follow the far stricter vegan diet, which excludes eggs and dairy products, too.

Some people choose vegetarianism because they are concerned about the welfare of animals raised for meat, along with the environmental consequences of meat production. Some want more complete information about the origin of their food. Others simply feel better eating an exclusively vegetarian diet.

Over the past 40 years the growing popularity of vegetarian cooking has been reflected in an ever more exciting range of recipes and produce. Here you will find more than 150 recipes, from light brunches to hearty main courses and delectable desserts, to inspire you to expand your vegetarian repertoire.

contents

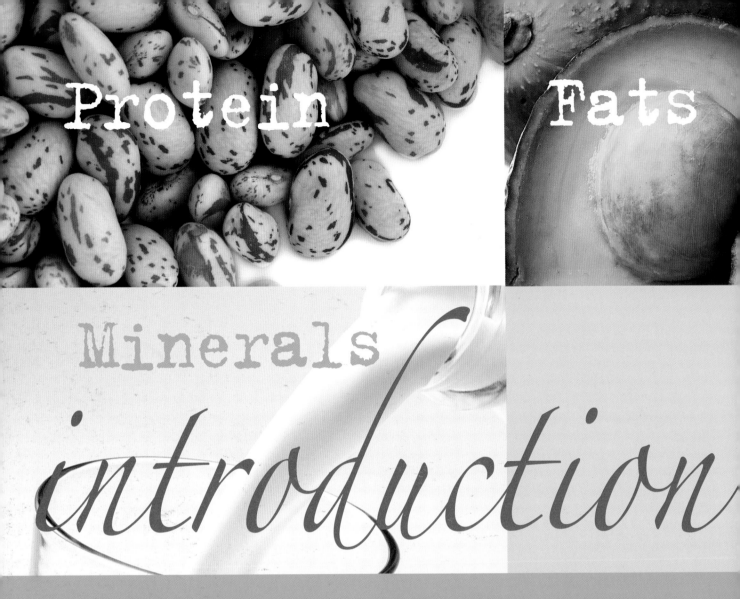

Protein

Fats

Minerals

introduction

A BALANCED DIET

As long as you eat a good variety of foods in the correct proportions, you should be able to achieve a healthy, balanced vegetarian diet. The basic rules are very simple—and apply whether or not you are following a vegetarian lifestyle. For general good health, eat plenty of complex carbohydrates, a wide variety of fruit and vegetables, and a small amount of protein. Add milk and dairy products for calcium (or their soy equivalents if you are vegan) but restrict saturated fat, salt, and sugar.

CARBOHYDRATES

Around half of your daily energy, or calories, should come from carbohydrates—but they should be the complex kind: starchy foods, such as brown rice, potatoes, and whole-wheat bread or pasta. These kinds of foods will make you feel full, keep you satisfied for longer, and provide you with a sustained source of energy. This last is particularly useful when doing sports or other energetic physical activity. Though sugary foods are also a source of carbohydrates, they tend to be calorie-rich with little other nutritional benefit. Restrict cakes, cookies, and other "empty calorie" carbohydrates to have as special treats.

FIBER

Fiber stimulates the digestive system and helps to prevent consti-pation, bowel disease, heart disease, and many other health problems. Add fiber with a variety of whole grains, including oats, as well as plenty of fruit and vegetables.

Vitamins

Carbohydrates

THE GLYCEMIC INDEX
The lower the GI (glycemic index) of a food, the more slowly it is digested and glucose released into the bloodstream. Low or medium GI foods will keep you fuller for longer and avoid the urge to snack.

PROTEIN
Dairy products, eggs, tofu, beans, and nuts are good sources of protein, which is needed for growth and repairing cells. The body does not need a lot of protein; around 45g a day is sufficient for most women, with 55g as a good average for men. Protein foods also contain valuable minerals, such as iron, zinc, and magnesium.

FATS
A small amount of fat makes food taste better and provides essential fatty acids and fat-soluble vitamins. Fat should form about one-third of a daily healthy diet. Current guidelines recommend cutting down on saturated fats as much as possible—not difficult with a vegetarian diet, since most are found in meat and dairy foods. Mono-unsaturated fat, found in nuts, olive oil, peanut oil, and avocados is a healthier source.

VITAMINS
Vitamins are the essential chemicals required by the body in small quantities to help repair, develop, and synthesize other nutrients. Raw fruit and vegetables tend to retain vitamins better because cooking can break down certain kinds of vitamins—particularly those from the B and C groups.

MINERALS
The body contains a number of minerals, around 20 of which are thought to be essential. Some, such as calcium, are needed in quite large quantities—more than 100mg a day. Others are known as trace minerals but are still important, although only required in small amounts.

◀ 1 medium apple

3 whole dried apricots ▶

▼ 1 medium banana

▲ 3 heaped
tablespoons
of carrots

◀ 2 broccoli florets

▼ 1 handful of grapes

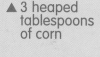

▲ 3 heaped
tablespoons
of corn

half a large ▶
zucchini

7 cherry
▼ tomatoes

▲ 7 strawberries

five a day

Current government advice is that everyone should eat at least five servings of fruit and vegetables a day. Each of the pictures shown above represents one of the five servings. But there is no harm in eating more than this, and it is positively beneficial to eat as varied a range as possible. It has been estimated that if everyone tried to eat their "five a day," the risk of deaths from chronic diseases such as heart disease, stroke, and cancer could be cut by as much as 20 percent. A recent study found that each serving of fruit and vegetables reduced the risk of heart disease by 4 percent and stroke by 6 percent. Other benefits may include delaying the onset of cataracts, reducing the symptoms of asthma, and improving the management of diabetes.

◄2 halves of canned peaches

2 satsumas ►

▲3 heaped tablespoons of cooked kidney beans

1 tablespoon of raisins ►

3 heaped ► tablespoons of peas

◄12 chunks of canned pineapple

1 medium glass of ► orange juice

▲1 handful of vegetable sticks

◄16 okra

1 medium pear ►

The government, along with the World Health Organization, recommends **that everyone eat** at least **five** servings of fresh vegetables and fruit every day.

vegetables

Vegetables are packed with vitamins and minerals. They also contain complex compounds known as phytochemicals. Some of these are antioxidants, which can destroy free radicals, playing a protective role against cancer—as well as other harmful effects. They are also one of the best sources of minerals, including iron, calcium, potassium, magnesium, and folate, and the vitamins A, B, C, and E. You will get far more nutritional benefit from eating vegetables for vitamins and minerals than you will from taking them as a supplement. Low in fat, calories, and cholesterol, vegetables are also an excellent source of dietary fiber—they will fill you up and keep your digestive system working smoothly.

BRASSICAS
Packed with minerals and vitamin C, brassicas include cabbage, kale, cauliflower, and the superfood broccoli.

BROCCOLI
Good in stir-fries, with pasta, in soufflés, or quiches. Remove coarse leaves before cooking and peel back woody stems. Raw or steamed broccoli retains the most nutrients.

CABBAGE AND KALE
Kale has loose leaves. Green and red cabbage form heads. Green and red cabbage work well as salads, while kale can be lightly steamed and served with butter as a side dish.

BRUSSELS SPROUTS
More strongly flavored than cabbage, they are generally eaten lightly cooked, although they can be used for salad. Remove outer leaves and cut a cross in the stem to help the sprouts cook more quickly.

FENNEL SEEDS

Aromatic fennel seeds are one of the world's oldest spices. Traditional medicines have used a fennel-based tea to help a range of digestive problems, from hiccups to colic. Fennel tea can also help to ease flatulence and bloating. In India toasted fennel seeds are chewed after a meal to prevent bad breath and aid digestion. In ancient Greece and Rome the seeds were eaten to prevent obesity. A teaspoon of cooled weak fennel tea can be used to soothe colicky infants.

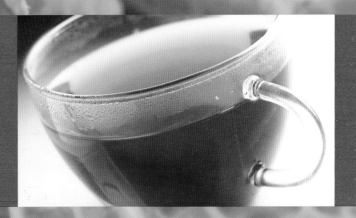

Vegetables, long relegated to a side dish, are finally being appreciated for their own flavor and texture and, most importantly, for their terrific health benefits.

CAULIFLOWER
Works well in curries and with cheese and cream sauces. Remove outer leaves and cut into florets before cooking. Slice stems thinly so they will cook more quickly.

LEAFY GREENS
Not always green, hues range from red or purple to dark bottle green.

SPINACH AND CHARD
Both work well in salads and soups. If using as an accompaniment, steam lightly in minimal water. Because they release so much water, you can expect the quantity to reduce by about half.

ASIAN GREENS
Loose leaved, they can be used in stir-fries and the young leaves in Asian salads. When preparing, chop the central rib and leaf separately.

STALKS AND BUDS
From artichokes to chicory, by way of asparagus, flavors range from delicate to more nutty or bitter.

GLOBE ARTICHOKE
A good source of folate and potassium, serve hot or cold with its leaves stripped down to the heart. To eat whole, cut off the top and boil in salted water for 30–40 minutes. The leaves should come away when pulled gently. Serve with vinaigrette or melted butter.

ASPARAGUS
Delicately flavored and tender at its best, asparagus was traditionally boiled upright in a tall saucepan. It is also wonderful grilled, roasted, or stir-fried.

CELERY
Great as a flavoring for soups and casseroles, celery also adds a crunchy bite to salads and stir-fries.

FENNEL
Use the aniseed flavor of fennel to accompany Italian ingredients, such as tomatoes and basil, or citrus fruits, apples, and pears. Slice thinly for salads or grill, roast, or steam.

Most vegetables can be eaten raw. If you prefer them cooked, microwave or steam to keep the nutrients.

SALAD VEGETABLES
The ultimate raw food, salad vegetables don't need cooking to be at their best.

LETTUCE
Enjoy a variety of lettuces, from mild butterhead to crisp romaine. Look for red varieties to add a touch of attractive color.

CUCUMBER
Mainly water, cucumber is a refreshing ingredient. It works well chopped in a yogurt dip or sliced into sticks for dipping.

AVOCADO
Actually a fruit, but with a delicate nutty flavor, avocados have a high fat content. It is healthy monounsaturated fat, though. Eat with a vinaigrette dressing or chop and add to salads. Ripe avocados will yield slightly when pressed and should peel with ease. Sprinkle with lemon juice when cut to keep them from going black.

RADISH
Little bulbs with crimson or white roots, radishes add a peppery flavor to salads.

MUSHROOMS
Eaten in quantity, mushrooms can be a good source of potassium and trace elements. But they tend to be used for taste and texture rather than nutrition.

FRESH OR DRY
Dried fungi have a more intense flavor than their fresh counterparts. They need to be soaked before use: rinse, cover with boiling water, and let stand for half an hour. Fresh mushrooms should be wiped.

BUTTON
These young mushrooms are ideal for salads, marinades, and stir-fries.

CHESTNUT
With a dense texture and stronger flavor, chestnut mushrooms are a good addition to stews, stronger-flavored sauces, nut roasts, and pie fillings.

CÈPE AND PORCINI
The French cèpe and Italian porcini are closely related. Available fresh or dried, they have a woody flavor.

SHIITAKE
Originally a wild native of Japan, it has a chewy texture and a strong flavor. Slice thinly for sauces and stir-fries and use in chunky pieces in casseroles.

PORTOBELLO
Substantial flat mushrooms that can be used as a base for a range of toppings. Broil, roast, stuff, or bake—or wrap in foil for the grill.

BEANS, PEAS, AND CORN
Colorful and crunchy, all are best at their freshest—although frozen versions are just as nutritious.

PEAS
Make the most of the short summer season for fresh peas. Choose smooth, unblemished pods, then pop the peas and lightly boil, steam, or microwave. Tiny fresh peas can be eaten raw.

SNOWPEAS
Edible pods containing immature peas, they add color and crunch to salads and stir-fries. Sugar snaps are the plumper versions.

BEANS
Green beans add color to casseroles and go well with Mediterranean vegetables, such as tomatoes, olives, and peppers. When served alone, they should be crisp and tender.

FAVA BEANS
Serve these substantial and nutritious beans with grain dishes, such as paella, and in garlicky salads.

CORN
Naturally sweet and delicious in all its forms. Use baby corn in stir-fries, cooked as corn on the cob or as kernels added to stews, grain dishes, or salads. Sharp flavors such as lime or chile add a bit of bite.

Try to vary the vegetables you **include in your "five a day"** to get the maximum range of nutrients.

ROOT VEGETABLES

Hearty and filling in soups and stews, root vegetables can be used in a huge variety of other ways.

CARROTS

Crunchy and sweet, raw carrots are a good source of beta carotene and dietary fiber. They are also excellent cooked in soups or as chunky pieces in casseroles, too.

POTATOES

Use waxy potatoes for salads, and baking potatoes for baking and mashing. They are a good source of starchy energy.

SWEET POTATOES

Their orange sweet-flavored flesh adds interest to casseroles and roasts well. Sweet potatoes are rich in vitamins.

PARSNIPS

With a sweet, strong flavor, parsnips are excellent roasted and make fantastic soup. They can be woody when older and should not be eaten raw.

TURNIPS

The best turnips are small and white with a greenish or purple tinge. They have a delicate peppery flavor. Young turnips don't need to be peeled. They can be used in casseroles, in mashes, steamed, sautéed, or stir-fried.

BEETS

Sweet and earthy, beets come in golden as well as red varieties. Scrub well, boil for 35–40 minutes, and then peel. Or roast or bake. They taste good cold in salads and are ideal for pickling.

JERUSALEM ARTICHOKE

Tasting a bit like water chestnuts, they are good in stews and soups and with cream or spices. Scrub and peel if necessary before cooking.

CELERY ROOT

A knobbly, warty plant with a delicate celery flavor. Good raw in salads, cooked in wine, or pureed with soft cheese.

RUTABAGAS

Peel to expose the yellow flesh and roast, steam, or microwave for maximum flavor.

CHILES

From mild to searingly hot, chiles add piquancy to a wide range of dishes. Mild sweet chiles make a delightful salad dish when roasted and peeled. Place in the oven or under a broiler and cook until the skin chars. The skin should come away easily; if not, place it in a plastic bag for 10 minutes. When preparing chiles, never touch your eyes or mouth.

VEGETABLE FRUITS

These colorful savory "fruits" can be cooked in a variety of ways and are excellent as stand-alones or added to casseroles and soups.

BELL PEPPERS

Mild relations of the spicy chile with a mild, sweet flavor. Excellent raw in salads, they can be stuffed, baked, and roasted. Like all bright red or orange vegetables, they are good sources of antioxidants.

EGGPLANT

A staple of Mediterranean, and especially Greek and Turkish cooking, they should feel glossy and heavy. Roast and puree or bake to prepare for inclusion in a moussaka.

ZUCCHINI

Do not skin. Wipe or rinse and chop large specimens. They can be stuffed, grilled, stir-fried, steamed lightly, or marinated for salads.

BUTTERNUT SQUASH

Use to add substance to casseroles or for colorful soups, or bake whole. They are good with cheese and strong spices or herbs to add flavor.

TOMATOES

Cherry or beefsteak work well raw in salads, while plum tomatoes are better for use in sauces and soups. Canned or sun-dried tomatoes are excellent for most cooking.

ONIONS

A key base flavoring for many dishes, onions may help to lower cholesterol levels and reduce the effect of fatty foods on the blood.

ONIONS AND SHALLOTS

Use sweet or red onions in salads. "Sweating" onions gives the flavor base for many soups and casseroles.

GARLIC

Adds a pungent flavor to a diverse range of cuisines. Chop or crush and be careful not to burn when cooking or it will become bitter.

LEEKS

When cooked slowly, leeks develop a delicate buttery texture. They are delicious with cheese and potatoes, in pies, casseroles, and soups.

> Keep a bowl of **apples, pears, or peaches** close at hand as a **healthy snack.** And buy berries in season when they are best in value and full of flavor.

fruit

Gorgeously colorful, sweetly juicy, and deliciously perfumed, there's a fruit for every taste. Make the most of local fruits in season as well as the exotic varieties now widely available. Most fruits are an important source of vitamin C, which cannot be stored in the body and needs a daily dose. Orange-fleshed fruits, including apricots, peaches, and mangoes, also contain antioxidant carotenes. You'll get the maximum nutritional benefit from the freshest fruit eaten raw. In addition to using fruits for desserts and snacks, it's worth incorporating fruit into savory dishes as well—apricots and dates will impart a Middle Eastern flavor to grain and rice-based recipes.

ORCHARD FRUITS
Delicious raw, apples and pears can also be cooked in a variety of ways for simple desserts.

APPLES
Apples are a good source of vitamin C, fiber, and bioflavonoids. Use cooking apples such as Rome Beauties for pies and sauces. Tart, crisp apples generally work best for cooking.

PEARS
With plenty of natural sugars, pears are a good energy-boosting food. They are also great stewed, grilled, or poached.

STONE FRUITS
Soft-fleshed with a large central pit, most are a good source of vitamin C and fiber, which aids digestion.

APRICOTS
Delicious dried, but also raw when completely ripe and poached for pies and crisps.

PEACHES
Buy firm but not rock hard, and ripen in a

BLUEBERRIES: A SUPERFRUIT

Naturally sweet, blueberries don't need cooking or sugar to make them palatable. Traditionally used to cure diarrhea and food poisoning, blueberries contain anthocyanins, which have antioxidant properties. They are a valuable aid against urinary tract infections, such as cystitis, and may also help to arrest deteriorating eyesight.

warm place. Poach, broil, grill, or stew and puree.

PLUMS
Black, red, purple, and yellow, some are grown specially for eating fresh, while others are best cooked. Brilliant in crisps and pies and dried as prunes.

CHERRIES
Naturally sweet, they are wonderful raw when in season. Also good in cakes or muffins or as purees and sauces.

GRAPES
Actually a vine fruit, grapes are at their best eaten raw and perfectly fresh. Darker varieties have a natural bloom.

BERRIES
Pick your own from the garden or a farm for the freshest seasonal berries. Strawberries and raspberries can be pureed without cooking.

STRAWBERRIES
Rich in antioxidants, they accompany most other fruits well. Fresh

purees, yogurts, and homemade ice cream are a refreshing summer treat.

RASPBERRIES
Always eat as soon as possible because raspberries are delicate and perishable. Buy frozen for purees.

BLACK AND RED CURRANTS
Tartly flavored, these tiny berries are an excellent topping for sweet, creamy desserts such as cheesecake. They are also packed with vitamin C.

CRANBERRIES
One of the superfruits, cranberries make a refreshing juice and excellent sauce for savory dishes. They may help to prevent urinary tract infections.

GOOSEBERRIES
Pale green or deep red, gooseberries need to be cooked and sweetened. They make good sauces and creamy purees.

All fruit is good for us, be it fresh, frozen, dried, or canned.

HEALTHY DESSERTS

Fruit is most beneficial when eaten raw. Combining a number of fruits in a fresh fruit salad is a simple way to achieve several servings of your "five a day" at one go. Prepare fruit salads at the last minute to retain maximum nutrients and keep them looking their best.

CITRUS FRUITS

With thick, fragrant skin and juice-packed flesh, citrus fruits are more durable than most and are a superb source of vitamin C. Many are used for their juice. Citrus juice also stops many other fruit and vegetables from turning brown when cut.

LEMONS

Sharply flavored, lemons make wonderful desserts when slightly sweetened and are also terrific used in savory dishes for added zest.

ORANGES

Use bitter oranges, such as the Seville, for marmalade and cooking; use sweet Valencia, naval, and blood oranges for eating alone. Blood oranges are particularly good in fruit salads.

THE ORANGE FAMILY

Mandarins, tangerines, satsumas, and clementines are related to oranges. Thinner-skinned and easier to peel, they generally are not used for cooking but are terrific in fruit salad.

GRAPEFRUITS

Slightly sour, grapefruits make a refreshing juice. They can be segmented for use in fruit salads or lightly broiled for a starter or breakfast dish—sprinkle a cut half with sugar and place under a preheated broiler for a few minutes.

KUMQUATS

Small oval fruits with an edible skin, they can be used as a garnish, with rice or couscous, and in savory salads.

TROPICAL FRUITS

A huge range of more exotic fruits is widely available.

BANANAS

A superb energy-blast food, bananas make a quick snack and are a rich source of potassium. They are delicious baked or broiled and used chopped in cakes.

DATES

Eat alone or stuff with a sweet or savory filling. Use dried in salads or Middle Eastern grain-based dishes.

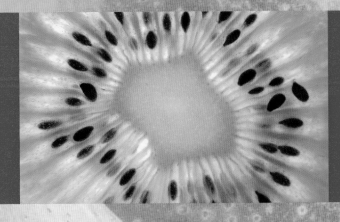

GETTING YOUR VITAMIN C

Many fruits are rich in vitamin C, vital for the production of collagen, an essential component of healthy skin, bones, cartilage, and teeth. It helps in healing wounds and burns and produces serotonin, which regulates sleep. Vitamin C improves the iron uptake of vegetarians because the iron in plant foods is absorbed more efficiently when eaten with foods or fruit juices containing vitamin C.

FIGS
The whole fruit is edible, including the skin and seeds. The sweet, delicate flavor of fresh figs is great with cheese. Dried figs are particularly high in fiber.

GUAVAS
Mix the pulpy pink flesh with soft cheese as a dip or combine with apples or pears in a pie or crisp.

KIWIFRUIT
The furry exterior belies the tempting brilliant green interior. Kiwis have a vitamin C content higher than oranges and are good on their own, as elegant toppings, or mixed with other fruits.

MANGOES
The rich, creamy flesh is great on its own or eaten with other fruits or in savory salads. Mango is also renowned for its beneficial effects on the skin and kidneys.

MELONS
Check a melon's ripeness by the sweetness of the smell. Combine with savories or eat alone or in a fruit salad.

PAPAYAS
With a yellow-green skin and pinky-orange flesh, papaya goes well with chiles, cilantro, and avocado but is good on its own with a little lime juice.

PASSION FRUITS
Inside its tough wrinkled exterior are a golden pulp and hundreds of edible seeds. Scoop out the seeds with a teaspoon or use the juice to flavor a fruit salad or fruit drink.

PINEAPPLES
Good in fruit salads and with savory ingredients, pineapple can be broiled and grilled and makes a lovely cake topping.

POMEGRANATES
Tightly packed seeds are surrounded by red flesh. Divide into four, and peel back the skin in sections to pull out the interior.

Supplying protein and many vitamins and minerals—in particular, calcium, milk, and other dairy products—can play a vital role in maintaining good health.

dairy

Dairy products, including milk, cheese, and yogurt, are a familiar starting point for those new to a vegetarian diet. A good source of protein and calcium, cow's milk contains vitamins, including A, B12, and D. Cheese in particular is high in saturated fat, so it should be eaten in moderation. Sheep and goat's milk products are also available and are an alternative for those who are sensitive to cow's milk. Eggs are also a great source of protein and are low in saturated fat. Choose free-range to ensure that they have been produced humanely. If you are looking for nondairy alternatives, soy can be processed into milk, cheese, and yogurt, while tahini and tofu can be used instead of eggs.

MILK
Whole and 1 or 2 percent milk have a higher vitamin and mineral content than skim. Those who cannot tolerate cow's milk can try goat's milk instead.

CRÈME FRAÎCHE
Rich, with a delicate tang, it is good as a dressing and works well in soups and sauces.

YOGURT
Made from cow's, sheep, and goat's milk and soy protein, yogurt is available set and in a more runny version. It is delicious in savory salad dressings and with fruit for desserts.

CHEESE
Unless you intend to be strictly vegan, it's hard to resist cheese. Choose varieties that are labeled as being suitable for vegetarians; this will ensure that they contain no rennet—an ingredient taken from a calf's stomach that is used to curdle and separate milk into curds and whey.

CHEDDAR
A firm-textured hard cheese; the aged varieties

ALTERNATIVES TO DAIRY

Soy milk does not taste like cow's milk but is fine as a drink or on cereals. It is not ideal for sauces because it does tend to curdle. Soy cheese has the texture of processed cheese and can seem rather fatty. Tahini is a good binding agent instead of eggs for burgers and casseroles but does curdle if you are not careful. Tofu can be used as an alternative to eggs in mayonnaise, while silken tofu can be scrambled.

will add lots of flavor to sauces, though milder ones are fine for toppings.

PARMESAN
There is no vegetarian version of traditional Parmesan. But a variety of Parmesan-style hard cheeses that don't contain rennet are available.

GRUYÈRE
A Swiss cheese with small holes, it is good for broiling and melts well.

FETA
A sharp-flavored sheep's milk cheese. Great in Mediterranean-style dishes and salads.

ROQUEFORT
A crumbly blue cheese made from sheep's milk.

STILTON
A classic English blue cheese, it should have a smooth, creamy texture. It is fantastic partnered with fresh figs.

BRIE
Look for a pale yellow center that is soft but

not runny. Good with fruit and in salads, but also delicious hot.

CHÈVRE
Goat's cheeses are strongly flavored and make lovely starters broiled and served with vegetables or salad.

RICOTTA
A whey-based Italian soft cheese with a light texture, it is often used as a filling for ravioli.

FROMAGE FRAIS
A soft unripened cheese, its slightly sharp taste is

often partnered with fruit in desserts.

MOZZARELLA
Firm-textured, it melts beautifully and is good with grilled vegetables and as a pizza topping.

EGGS
Store in the refrigerator with the pointed end downward to keep the yolk centered. Test for freshness by using the "float" test; a fresh egg will sink. If using separated eggs, use yolks within a couple of days and whites within a week.

COOKING RICE AND WHOLE GRAINS

Bring a large saucepan of water to a boil. Add the grain and bring back to a boil, then simmer gently until the grain is tender. Drain well. For risotto rice, millet, and short-grain rice, use 4 cups stock for 1⅓ cups grain. Add a third of the stock and bring to a boil, stirring constantly. When all the stock has been absorbed, repeat the process with the next third and finally the last third of the stock. The whole process should take 20–30 minutes.

grains and

Cereals and grains are staples of many diets, from wheat, rye, and barley in temperate zones to rice, corn, and millet in more tropical climes. Whole grains are seeds and contain a variety of valuable nutrients, including carbohydrates, fiber, and essential amino acids. Once the grain is processed and the outer layer is cracked or removed, it begins to lose its nutritional value. Lesser-known grains, such as quinoa, buckwheat, and wild rice, offer exciting alternatives.

Pasta can be made from any kind of flour and processed into a huge variety of shapes and sizes. Choose whole-wheat pasta for slow-release energy and cook lightly to maintain authentic al dente texture.

WHOLE GRAINS

Grains are a rich source of essential amino acids and, eaten in conjunction with beans or nuts, will provide a complete vegetarian protein. They also contain valuable minerals.

BARLEY

One of the most ancient grains, barley today tends to be added to soups and casseroles.

MILLET

With a milder flavor than rice, the round grains of millet can be used for both sweet and savory dishes.

QUINOA

Round grains with a delicate grassy flavor make an excellent accompaniment for spicy vegetable dishes. Do not overcook.

BUCKWHEAT

A flavorful grain, it is sometimes known as kasha when toasted. Buckwheat goes well with root vegetables, mushrooms, and dark green vegetables.

OATS

Used mainly in the form of flakes, oats are the basis of granola and

THE GI FACTOR

Pasta is one of the best sources of slow-release carbohydrates—it's still recommended as being one of the best foods to eat the night before running a marathon. It is also low in fat and a useful source of protein. To get the maximum slow-release energy from your pasta, it should be cooked until it is just beginning to soften, not until soft or soggy.

Grains, pasta, and rice are some of the most versatile ingredients in a vegetarian diet. Always keep a selection in the pantry as an essential standby.

pasta

oatmeal. The soluble dietary fiber they contain is thought to lower blood cholesterol.

RICE
Many different varieties are now available. Keep a selection and choose the kind that best suits your recipe.

SHORT-GRAIN
These round, sticky grains are suitable for savory stuffings, puddings, and risotto-style dishes.

LONG-GRAIN
Long-grain brown rice is nutty and good with

chili, stir-fries, and curries.

BASMATI
Fragrant, with long, slender grains, it is a natural partner for curries and a range of other dishes.

RISOTTO
As the starch breaks down, the rice attains its creamy quality; varieties include arborio and carnaroli.

RED RICE
A Mediterranean rice with russet-colored grains that are nutty and

chewy, it is good with other kinds of rice and with vegetables.

WILD RICE
The long slender grains are dark brown and have a nutty flavor that goes well with nuts and vegetables such as peppers and tomatoes.

WHEAT
BULGUR
Made from cooked, dried, and cracked whole wheat, it must be soaked in boiling water before using.

COUSCOUS
Made from the inner layers of the wheat, it can be lightly steamed or soaked in boiling water for 5 minutes.

PASTA
Keep pasta in a wide range of sizes, shapes, and thicknesses. Added flavors such as tomato, spinach, basil, chile, and egg also add variety. Fine pastas are best with light, smooth sauces, while shells, curls, and broad noodles are usually better with chunkier sauces.

Almost all of the beans contain **a near-perfect balance** of starchy carbohydrate and protein.

Dried peas, beans, and lentils are a cheap and nutritious alternative to meat. They contain some protein, but not all the amino acids essential for growth and the maintenance of healthy tissues. To get a good balance, serve with vegetables and whole grains, such as rice or bread. Soybeans are the exception and are classed as a high-quality protein. Beans are also an excellent source of dietary fiber and generally have a low GI, so they will keep you full for longer. Nuts are a great source of energy. Though they are high in fat and calories, they contain essential fatty acids and are a good source of B vitamins, which vegetarians may have difficulty obtaining.

BEANS AND LENTILS

Beans and lentils can be the basis for soups, stews, and casseroles as well as burgers. They will make a salad or a pasta sauce more substantial. And they are one of the cheapest forms of protein available.

BEANS

Dried beans have a long shelf life but should look plump and glossy, not wrinkled or cracked. Use black or kidney beans with chiles, mung beans with Indian spices, cannellini beans with Mediterranean flavors, and chickpeas for a Middle Eastern taste. To make beans more digestible, change the water during soaking, cook with spices such as cumin or caraway, and try sprouting for a day or so before cooking.

LENTILS

Lentils go well with beans and are superb in soups and casseroles and as the basis for a hearty salad. They mix well with a huge range of different ingredients,

PREPARING DRIED BEANS

All beans contain a toxin called lectin. Soaking and cooking are essential to render it harmless. To long-soak, place in a large bowl and cover with four times their volume in cold water. Soy beans and chickpeas may need to soak for eight hours or overnight until they appear plump. To quick soak, bring the beans to a boil in a saucepan containing four times their volume in water. Boil for 3–5 minutes, then leave to stand for an hour.

COOKING TIMES FOR BEANS	LENGTH OF COOKING TIME MAY VARY ACCORDING TO QUANTITY, SO THESE ARE GUIDELINES ONLY.
VARIETY	COOKING TIME
MUNG, FLAGEOLET	45–50 MINUTES
ADUKI, BLACK-EYE, BORLOTTI, CANNELLINI, PINTO	50–60 MINUTES
HARICOT	60–70 MINUTES
BLACK, BUTTER, LIMA, CHICKPEA, RED KIDNEY	60–90 MINUTES
SOYBEANS	UP TO 4 HOURS

nuts

both sweet and savory. Lentils just need picking over and rinsing before cooking. For whole lentils, bring to a boil and cook until just soft. With split lentils, used for purees or sauces, measure the water exactly to avoid a gloopy mixture: 2 cups lentils to 6 cups water is a useful guide.

NUTS AND SEEDS

To add extra flavor, texture, and nutritional value to a wide range of dishes, add some nuts. They contain healthy polyunsaturated fats, as well as iron, zinc, and magnesium. Roasting nuts and seeds enhances their flavor. Spread in a shallow baking sheet and roast in the oven at 400°F for 6–10 minutes.

PISTACHIOS

Delicious in savory grain dishes and salads and in ice cream where the slight almond flavor will be obvious.

WALNUTS

The strong flavor makes walnuts a good base for roasts and burgers. They are good in salads and with grains, as well as adding crunch to cakes and breads.

PINE NUTS

Serve lightly toasted in salads or with roasted vegetables. They work well with tomatoes and peppers and are a key ingredient of pesto sauces.

CASHEWS

Mild but distinctive, cashews are good with rice and stir-fries and with aromatic spices.

CHESTNUTS

Low in fat compared to other nuts, they are useful in roasts and casseroles. Their slightly sweet flavor can be seasoned with herbs or soy sauce. When soaking dried chestnuts, keep the leftover stock to use as a base for soups.

SEEDS

Sunflower, sesame, and pumpkin seeds add texture and flavor to salads, breads, and dressings. All can be toasted or eaten raw.

brea

fast
and brunch

BREAKFAST AND BRUNCH

CORN CAKES WITH YOGURT SAUCE

These pancakes make a delicious Sunday breakfast treat; they are also good as a light lunch with a crispy green salad or served as a side dish with a main meal.

⅝ cup (75g) cornmeal
⅝ cup (75g) white bread flour
2 teaspoons baking powder
Salt and black pepper
1 tablespoon vegetable oil, plus extra for greasing the pan
⅝ cup (150ml) skim milk or water
1 ear fresh corn, or 1 cup (125g) canned corn or frozen corn, defrosted
2 tablespoons chopped fresh cilantro
2 egg whites

FOR THE SAUCE
6 ounces (150g) low-fat Greek-style yogurt
Grated zest of 1 lemon
1 tablespoon lemon juice
2 tablespoons chopped fresh cilantro

PREPARATION TIME 5 minutes, plus
  20 minutes standing
COOKING TIME 20 minutes
MAKES 12

1 Combine the cornmeal, flour, baking powder, and some black pepper in a large bowl. Add the oil and the milk, and stir until the batter has a thick, dropping consistency. 2 If using fresh corn, cut off the tip and stand the cob upright on a cutting board. Hold it firmly by the stem and, using a sharp knife, slice off the kernels, following the hard cob as your guide. Add the corn kernels and cilantro to the batter, mix well, cover, and allow to rest for 20 minutes. 3 Whisk the egg whites and a pinch of salt into soft peaks. Add a little beaten white to the batter to loosen it, then fold in the rest. 4 Heat a griddle or large frying pan and spread a thin coating of oil over it with a piece of paper towel. Keep the paper towel on hand and use it to grease the pan for the next batch. 5 Dip a large tablespoon in water and use it to drop spoonfuls of the batter onto the hot griddle. Cook for 2–3 minutes until browned, then turn them over and cook for another 3–4 minutes. Keep the first batch warm and repeat until all the batter has been used, greasing the griddle or pan after each batch. 6 To make the sauce, mix all the ingredients in a bowl and serve with the pancakes.

NUTRIENTS PER SERVING CAL 760 • CARBOHYDRATE 12g (sugars 1g) • PROTEIN 3g • FAT 2g (saturated fat 0.1g) • FIBER 0.5g • SODIUM 114mg

APPLE AND CHEESE TOASTS

Cut thick slices from a large loaf of good whole-wheat bread for this fruity version of grilled cheese, where a sweet layer of dessert apple lies hidden beneath the golden topping.

2 small red apples
4 thick slices whole-wheat bread
5 ounces (150g) Cheddar, Cheshire, or Emmental cheese
Butter for spreading
8 sage leaves
Black pepper

TOTAL TIME 15 minutes
MAKES 4

1 Preheat the broiler. Quarter the apples, then core and thinly slice them. **2** Toast the bread on one side under the broiler. Meanwhile, finely slice or grate the cheese. **3** Turn the bread over and spread the untoasted side with butter. Arrange the apple slices on top and cover with cheese. Broil for 4–5 minutes, until the cheese melts and the apples heat through. **4** Meanwhile, finely chop the sage leaves. When the toasts are ready, sprinkle them with the chopped sage and black pepper and serve immediately.

NUTRIENTS PER SERVING CAL 327 • CARBOHYDRATE 26g (sugars 8g) • PROTEIN 14g • FAT 18g (saturated fat 11g) • FIBER 3.5g • SODIUM 545mg

Apples are a good source of vitamin C, which is an antioxidant and helps to maintain the immune system.

GLAMORGAN SAUSAGES

Instead of meat, Glamorgan sausages are made with cheese, which, as the Welsh name suggests, should be Caerphilly. Celery has been added to lighten the texture and add a little crunch.

FOR THE WATERCRESS SAUCE
2 ounces (70g) watercress
6 ounces (175g) low-fat cream cheese, softened
Salt and black pepper

2 thin celery ribs, white part only, very finely chopped
3¾ cups (175g) fresh whole-wheat bread crumbs
4 ounces (115g) Caerphilly cheese, finely grated
1 tablespoon chopped fresh parsley
Black pepper
1 large egg, beaten
About 2 tablespoons milk
All-purpose flour for shaping
Olive oil for brushing

PREPARATION TIME 10 minutes
COOKING TIME 5 minutes
SERVES 4

1 For the watercress sauce, bring a saucepan of water to a boil, add the watercress, and return to a boil. Drain at once, pressing out excess moisture with the back of a spoon. Chop finely, then put in a bowl. Add the cream cheese and mix well. Add salt and pepper to taste and set aside. **2** Combine the celery, bread crumbs, cheese, and parsley in a bowl. Add black pepper and stir to mix. Using a fork, quickly mix in the egg and just enough milk to bind the mixture. **3** Divide the mixture into eight. Using floured hands, lightly roll each piece into a sausage shape about 4 inches (10cm) long. **4** Preheat the broiler and lightly brush the sausages with oil. Broil the sausages for about 5 minutes, until golden brown, turning them occasionally. Serve with the watercress sauce.

NUTRIENTS PER SERVING CAL 320 • CARBOHYDRATE 21g (sugars 3g) • PROTEIN 17g • FAT 20g (saturated fat 10g) • FIBER 3g • SODIUM 412mg

CRUSHED BEANS ON TOAST

A sophisticated fresh-flavored version of the British snack, using butter beans instead of the navy beans traditionally used in many recipes—an excellent source of protein, minerals, and fiber.

4 cloves garlic
5 tablespoons olive oil
Handful of fresh flat-leaved parsley
Salt and black pepper
15-ounce (400g) can butter or lima beans, drained and rinsed
1 small onion, finely chopped
1 bay leaf
2–3 teaspoons fresh thyme leaves
2 slices of bread, toasted

PREPARATION TIME 5 minutes
COOKING TIME 10 minutes
SERVES 2

1 Put the garlic into a small saucepan, cover with water, and simmer for 5 minutes. Drain and put into a blender with 4 tablespoons of the oil and the parsley. Blend to a puree, add salt and pepper to taste, and set aside. **2** Meanwhile, heat the remaining 1 tablespoon oil in a saucepan. Add the beans, onion, bay leaf, and thyme and cook for 2–3 minutes, crushing the beans coarsely with a fork, until warmed through. Discard the bay leaf. **3** Add salt and pepper to taste and pile the beans onto the toast. Top with the parsley sauce and serve.

NUTRIENTS PER SERVING CAL 500 • CARBOHYDRATE 47g (sugars 6g) • PROTEIN 15g • FAT 29g (saturated fat 4g) • FIBER 10g • SODIUM 1023mg

SPICY SCRAMBLED EGGS ON TOAST

Scrambled eggs become a tasty treat when cooked with fresh herbs, spices, and a splash of lime juice. This dish holds its own as a late-night snack, too.

4 thick slices of whole-wheat bread
1 tablespoon butter
1 green chile, seeded and diced
2 teaspoons curry paste
1 clove garlic, crushed
1 teaspoon grated fresh ginger
4 scallions, chopped
3 ounces (85g) tomatoes, peeled and diced
6 eggs
1 tablespoon chopped fresh cilantro
1 teaspoon lime juice
Salt and black pepper
4 tablespoons low-fat plain yogurt, optional

PREPARATION TIME 15 minutes
COOKING TIME 8–10 minutes
SERVES 4

1 Toast the bread and keep it warm. **2** Melt the butter in a nonstick frying pan and add the chile, curry paste, garlic, ginger, and scallions, reserving a few for a garnish. Fry them over low heat for 5 minutes, until softened but not browned. Stir in the tomatoes and cook for another minute. **3** Beat the eggs with the cilantro, lime juice, and salt and pepper to taste. Add the eggs to the pan and stir gently over a low heat until just set. **4** Lay the toast on plates, top with the curried eggs, sprinkle with the reserved scallions, and add some yogurt if you wish.

**NUTRIENTS PER SERVING CAL 272 • CARBOHYDRATE 17g (sugars 4g) • PROTEIN 17g
• FAT 16g (saturated fat 5g) • FIBER 2g • SODIUM 399mg**

EGG-WHITE OMELET WITH ASPARAGUS

The delicate flavor of asparagus replaces the taste of egg yolk in this feather-light, low-calorie, low-cholesterol omelet. If asparagus is out of season, use baby spinach or broccoli instead.

3–4 ounces (100g) asparagus, trimmed, or asparagus tips
Salt and black pepper
4 egg whites
½ teaspoon sunflower oil

PREPARATION TIME 10 minutes
COOKING TIME 16 minutes
SERVES 1

1 Put a steamer on to boil, then steam the asparagus for 8 minutes, or until tender, and drain. Season to taste while still warm. **2** Whisk the egg whites until frothy but not forming peaks: The mixture should be pourable. Do not add salt, because it will break down the froth. **3** Heat the oil in a small nonstick omelet pan or frying pan, swirling it around until it covers the bottom with a thin film. Pour in the omelet mixture and cook over a low to medium heat for 2–3 minutes, until the bottom is firm. **4** Slide the omelet onto a plate. Lay the asparagus in the pan, then carefully invert the omelet on top. Cook for another 2–3 minutes, until the bottom has just set and the asparagus is golden brown, then serve.

NUTRIENTS PER SERVING CAL 89 • CARBOHYDRATE 2g (sugars 2g) • PROTEIN 14g • FAT 3g (saturated fat 0.5g) • FIBER 1.5g • SODIUM 244mg

snacks and

tarters

SNACKS AND STARTERS

AVOCADO AND WATERCRESS DIP

A blend of creamy avocado and spicy watercress, this pretty puree can be eaten with a teaspoon or served as a dip. Watercress is an excellent source of vitamins C and E—and it tastes great, too.

1 bunch of watercress
A few sprigs of parsley
A few scallions
1 clove garlic
1 lemon
A few basil leaves
4 tablespoons olive oil

2 large avocados
Salt and black pepper
1 tablespoon green peppercorns in brine

TOTAL TIME 18 minutes
SERVES 4

1 Discard the stems from the watercress. Strip the parsley leaves from the stems. **2** Chop the green tops of the scallions, leaving the whites for another dish, and put them into a blender or food processor with the parsley and watercress. **3** Peel the garlic and crush it into the parsley and watercress. Wash any wax from the lemon, grate the rind, squeeze out the juice, and add both to the blender or processor. Chop a few basil leaves and set them aside for a garnish. Add the remaining leaves to the mixture with the olive oil. **4** Halve and pit the avocados. Leaving the shells intact, spoon the flesh into the blender or food processor and season. Process until smooth. **5** Spoon the puree into the avocado shells, sprinkle it with the peppercorns and reserved basil, and serve.

NUTRIENTS PER SERVING CAL 300 • CARBOHYDRATE 2.5g (sugars 1g) • PROTEIN 3g • FAT 30g (saturated fat 6g) • FIBER 4g • SODIUM 19mg

The flesh of a ripe **avocado** is as good for you as it tastes.

EGGPLANT PÂTÉ

Warm eggplant pâté packed with herbs and spices makes a fine smoky-flavored dish to start a meal or serve as a snack. Served hot or cold, it tastes wonderful and can be made in advance.

2 tablespoons olive oil
1 medium onion, finely chopped
1 large, firm eggplant
10 sun-dried tomatoes
6 small gherkins
3 cloves garlic, minced
A few sprigs of thyme
A few sprigs of parsley

1 teaspoon whole-grain mustard
1 teaspoon balsamic vinegar
2 teaspoons capers
1 loaf French bread
Salt and black pepper

TOTAL TIME 30 minutes
SERVES 4

1 Heat the oil over medium heat in a frying pan. Add the onion and sauté for 5 minutes, or until soft. **2** Cut the eggplant into ½-inch (1cm) cubes. Add them to the onion and sauté for 8–10 minutes, or until they have softened. **3** Drain and chop the sun-dried tomatoes and the gherkins and add them to the eggplant with the garlic. **4** Strip the leaves from the thyme and parsley and chop finely. Reserve some parsley for a garnish and add the rest of the herbs to the pan, with the mustard, vinegar, and capers. Simmer, stirring frequently, for 5 minutes. **5** Meanwhile, cut and toast the French bread. **6** Season the eggplant mixture with salt and pepper, then blend it in a food processor or mash it to a paste by hand. **7** Spoon the pâté onto individual plates, sprinkle with the reserved parsley, and serve with the toast.

NUTRIENTS PER SERVING CAL 357 • CARBOHYDRATE 55g (sugars 8g) • PROTEIN 10g • FAT 12g (saturated fat 1g) • FIBER 4g • SODIUM 694mg

CHEESE AND MUSHROOM PÂTÉ

This is a very good way of using up scraps of leftover vegetarian cheese, as well as making a healthy, satisfying snack or lunch. Mushrooms add a wonderful flavor and texture to the dish.

1 tablespoon unsalted butter
5 large, flat mushrooms, about 8 ounces (22g), roughly chopped
1 large leek, trimmed and finely chopped
5 tablespoons half-fat crème fraîche
1 teaspoon English mustard
Pinch of freshly grated nutmeg

Black pepper
4 ounces (125g) Cheddar or Lancashire cheese, crumbled

PREPARATION TIME 10 minutes, plus 1 hour chilling
COOKING TIME 10 minutes
SERVES 4

1 Melt the butter over medium heat in a large saucepan. Add the mushrooms and leek, cover, and cook for 5 minutes, stirring occasionally. Add the crème fraîche, mustard, nutmeg, and some black pepper and cook, uncovered, for 5 minutes, until almost all the liquid has evaporated.
2 Transfer the mixture to a blender or food processor, add the cheese, and puree in short bursts until smooth. **3** Scrape the mixture into a bowl or four individual ramekins and chill for at least 1 hour or overnight before serving.

NUTRIENTS PER SERVING CAL 200 • CARBOHYDRATE 2g (sugars 1g) • PROTEIN 10g • FAT 16g (saturated fat 11g) • FIBER 1g • SODIUM 236mg

Mushrooms are a good source of potassium and some trace elements, especially copper.

BRANDIED CHESTNUT AND MUSHROOM TERRINE

The chestnuts in this flavor-packed dish contain only a fraction of the fat in most other nuts.

1 tablespoon olive oil
2–4 cloves garlic, crushed
6 ounces (175g) mushrooms, sliced
1 small red onion, thinly sliced
6 tablespoons brandy
8 vacuum-packed or canned unsweetened,
  whole chestnuts
1 egg, beaten
1¼ cups (125g) whole-grain bread crumbs
1 14-ounce (400g) can unsweetened chestnut
  puree

Grated zest of ½ orange plus juice of 1 orange
1 tablespoon each chopped fresh parsley
  and thyme
Salt and black pepper

TO GARNISH chopped fresh cilantro or basil
TO SERVE mixed salad greens

PREPARATION TIME 20 minutes
COOKING TIME 55 minutes
SERVES 8–10

1 Preheat the oven to 350°F. Lightly oil a 2-pound (900g) loaf pan. **2** Heat the oil in a large saucepan over medium heat and sauté the garlic, mushrooms, and onions for 7–8 minutes, until they are tender and lightly browned, stirring frequently. **3** Add the brandy to the pan and allow it to simmer for 1–2 minutes until reduced. Remove the pan from the heat and leave the mixture to cool for about 3 minutes. **4** Break the chestnuts into pieces and stir them into the mushroom mixture with the egg, bread crumbs, chestnut puree, orange zest and juice, parsley, thyme, and salt and pepper to taste, using a wooden spoon to break up the chestnut puree. **5** When the mixture is thoroughly combined, spoon it into the loaf pan, smooth over the top, and bake it for 45 minutes, or until the top is browned. **6** Leave the terrine to cool in the pan, then turn it out onto a plate and cut it into neat slices. Sprinkle a little chopped cilantro over the top and serve it with the salad greens.

NUTRIENTS PER SERVING CAL 234 • CARBOHYDRATE 38g (sugars 6g) • PROTEIN 6g • FAT 4g (saturated fat 1g) • FIBER 4g • SODIUM 97mg

GARLICKY FLAGEOLET BEAN TERRINE

Wrapped in shining green grape leaves and studded with stuffed green olives, this creamy terrine is a real winner. Serve it with crisp endive, fresh orange segments, and crusty French bread for an unusual and attractive starter.

8 ounces (225g) dried flageolet or cannellini beans, soaked for at least 8 hours
1 small onion, halved
Strip of lemon zest
2 bay leaves
10 grape leaves preserved in brine, or as needed
½ cup (115g) cottage cheese
2 garlic cloves, crushed
1 tablespoon lemon juice
2 eggs, lightly beaten
2 tablespoons chopped fresh parsley
16 pimiento-stuffed green olives, sliced
Salt and black pepper

TO SERVE 1 small head Belgian endive, leaves separated
2 oranges, peeled and segmented
2 ounces (45g) almonds, toasted

PREPARATION AND COOKING TIME 2¾ hours, plus 6–8 hours soaking and 2 hours chilling
SERVES 8

1 Drain the soaked beans and rinse under cold running water. Combine them in a saucepan with the onion, lemon zest, bay leaves, and enough cold water to cover generously. Bring to a boil and boil rapidly for 10 minutes, then reduce the heat and simmer for 45–60 minutes, until tender. **2** Meanwhile, drain the grape leaves and rinse them in cold water. Spread out on paper towels and pat dry. Lightly oil a 2-pound (900g) terrine dish or loaf pan and line it with the grape leaves, shiny side out, allowing them to hang over the top of the dish. Set aside. **3** Preheat the oven to 350°F (180°C). Drain the beans and discard the onion, lemon zest, and bay leaves. Pour the beans into a bowl and mash with a potato masher until fairly smooth. **4** Add the cottage cheese, garlic, lemon juice, eggs, parsley, and salt and pepper to taste. Mix together, then fold in the olives. Spoon into the prepared terrine dish, pressing the mixture into the corners. Level the top, then fold over the overhanging leaves. Cover with additional leaves, if necessary. **5** Cover the top of the dish with a piece of oiled aluminum foil, tucking the edges under the rim to seal securely. Set the dish in a roasting pan and pour enough warm water into the pan to come two-thirds of the way up the sides of the dish. Bake for 1 hour, or until the top of the terrine feels firm to the touch. Remove the dish from the water, set it on a wire rack, and leave to cool. Chill for at least 2 hours before serving. **6** To unmold, run a knife around the edges of the terrine and turn out onto a plate or board. Cut into slices and transfer to plates. Garnish each serving with endive leaves, orange segments, and almonds.

NUTRIENTS PER SERVING CAL 177 • CARBOHYDRATE 15g (sugars 6g) • PROTEIN 13g • FAT 8g (saturated fat 2g) • FIBER 9g • SODIUM 203mg

FRESH HERB DIP WITH CHICKPEA CRÊPES

A feast of summery herbs is packed into this lemon-flavored dip, served with tasty little pancakes.

FOR THE HERB DIP
A few sprigs each of basil, chives, dill,
 and/or parsley
1 cup (200ml) crème fraîche
½ lemon
1 small clove garlic, minced
Salt and black pepper

FOR THE CRÊPES
1 cup (115g) chickpea flour
1 cup (115g) all-purpose flour
2 tablespoons olive oil
1¾ cups (400ml) lukewarm water

TOTAL TIME 30 minutes
SERVES 4

1 To make the herb dip, finely chop enough herbs to make 4 tablespoons. Put the herbs into a small bowl with the crème fraîche and 1 tablespoon of lemon juice. Add the garlic, mix well, and add salt and pepper to taste. **2** To make the crêpes, combine the chickpea and all-purpose flours in a bowl. Add the oil and water gradually, whisking until the batter is smooth. Transfer to a measuring cup. **3** Heat a 6-inch (15cm) nonstick frying pan over high heat, then pour in just under ¼ cup (50ml) of the batter, tilting the pan so it covers the bottom evenly. Cook the crêpe for 30 seconds, or until golden, then flip it over and cook the other side for about 15 seconds. **4** Turn the crêpe onto a plate and roll it up. Keep it warm while you cook and roll the rest of the crêpes, then cut them in half and serve with the dip.

NUTRIENTS PER SERVING CAL 429 • CARBOHYDRATE 38g (sugars 3g) • PROTEIN 10g • FAT 27g (saturated fat 14g) • FIBER 4g • SODIUM 23mg

Garlic and other members of the onion family may help to lower blood pressure and blood cholesterol.

Eggs are an excellent source of vitamin B12, which is vital for the healthy functioning of the nervous system.

CROWDIE EGGS

Crowdie is a Scottish fresh cheese, traditionally made by crofters. The name comes from the Lowland Scots word "cruds," meaning curds. Serve with crackers.

5 cups (1.2l) skim milk
Juice of ½ lemon
Salt and black pepper
3 large hard-cooked eggs, peeled
    and finely chopped
Grated zest of 1 lemon
1 tablespoon each finely
    chopped chives and chervil

1 tablespoon low-fat mayonnaise
2 scallions, finely chopped

PREPARATION TIME 10 minutes, plus cooling
    and chilling
COOKING TIME 12 minutes
SERVES 4

1 Pour the milk into a bowl and add the lemon juice. Leave to stand for 20–30 minutes, until soured. Transfer to a saucepan and place over a very low heat until just warm, but not simmering, and the liquid whey separates from the curds. Remove from the heat and leave to cool, then drain off the whey. 2 Line a colander with a clean dish towel. Pour in the curds and leave until most of the remaining whey has drained. Gather up the corners of the cloth and squeeze out the last of the liquid. Transfer to a bowl—there should be about 4 ounces (140g). Add a pinch of salt, beat until smooth, and set aside. 3 Put the chopped egg into a bowl with the lemon zest, chives, chervil, mayonnaise, and pepper. 4 Fold the eggs into the curds until mixed. Spoon into four ramekins and sprinkle with the scallions. Chill for 30 minutes, then serve.

NUTRIENTS PER SERVING CAL 174 • CARBOHYDRATE 14g (sugars 14g) • PROTEIN 16g
• FAT 7g (saturated fat 2g) • FIBER 0g • SODIUM 232mg

ROASTED ASPARAGUS WITH CARAMELIZED SHALLOT DRESSING

Roasting asparagus is a healthier alternative to drenching it in butter. For a smoky flavor, cook lightly oiled asparagus on the grill, turning the spears once or twice.

1 pound (500g) asparagus, trimmed
4 teaspoons olive oil
6 large cloves garlic
4 shallots
3 tablespoons balsamic vinegar
Salt and black pepper
1 tablespoon chopped fresh thyme, sage, and
   rosemary mixed, or all thyme

PREPARATION TIME 10 minutes, plus 2–3 hours
   cooling, optional
COOKING TIME 20 minutes
SERVES 4

1 Preheat the oven to 450°F (230°C). 2 Place the asparagus in an ovenproof dish, drizzle with 2 teaspoons of the oil, and use your fingers to rub it in so that all the spears are well coated. Roast the asparagus for 15–20 minutes, depending on the thickness of the spears, until they have softened and browned slightly. 3 Meanwhile, peel and quarter the garlic and shallots. Heat the remaining 2 teaspoons of the oil in a wok or heavy pan over high heat. Add the garlic and shallots and stir-fry for 5–7 minutes until they are golden brown. 4 Add 4 tablespoons water, reduce the heat, cover, and simmer for 10–15 minutes, until softened. Then increase the heat and boil until most of the water has evaporated. 5 Add the vinegar and bring to a boil, then pour the dressing over the hot asparagus. Season with salt and pepper to taste, and sprinkle with the herbs. Serve immediately or set aside for a few hours to allow the flavors to develop, then serve at room temperature.

NUTRIENTS PER SERVING CAL 76 • CARBOHYDRATE 6g (sugars 6g) • PROTEIN 4g • FAT 4g (saturated fat 0.5g) • FIBER 2.5g • SODIUM 2mg

TURKISH EGGPLANT WITH TOMATO AND YOGURT SAUCE

Flavorful spoonfuls of yogurt, tomato, and toasted cumin seeds make a tasty partner for slices of smoky eggplant cooked with very little fat.

1¼ pounds (600g) eggplant
2 tablespoons olive oil
2 teaspoons cumin seeds
½ cup (100g) canned chopped tomatoes
4 ounces (100g) low-fat plain yogurt
Salt and black pepper

TO GARNISH fresh cilantro leaves

PREPARATION TIME 10 minutes
COOKING TIME 15 minutes, plus cooling
SERVES 4

1 Heat a ridged cast-iron grill pan over medium-high heat. Cut the eggplant widthwise into 12 thick slices, discarding the ends. Lightly brush both sides of each slice with oil and cook for 3–4 minutes on each side, until the flesh is soft when pierced. Alternatively, you can cook the eggplant slices under a hot broiler. **2** Set the cooked eggplant slices aside to cool; they taste best at room temperature. **3** Meanwhile, heat a small frying pan over high heat. Dry-fry the cumin seeds for a few seconds, or until they turn dark brown. Remove them from the pan immediately and set aside. When they are cool, grind them to a powder in a spice mill or with a pestle and mortar. **4** Put the tomatoes in a saucepan and cook over medium heat for 3–4 minutes, stirring occasionally, until they are reduced to a thick sauce, then set aside to cool. **5** When the tomato sauce has cooled, add the ground spice and yogurt, mix together, and season to taste. If you have time, chill the sauce a little. **6** To serve, lay three slices of the char-grilled eggplant on each of four plates and add a spoonful of the tomato and yogurt sauce along the side of each. Garnish with a few fresh cilantro leaves and serve.

NUTRIENTS PER SERVING CAL 89 • CARBOHYDRATE 6g (sugars 2.5g) • PROTEIN 3g • FAT 6g (saturated fat 1g) • FIBER 3g • SODIUM 29mg

WILD MUSHROOMS AND BLUEBERRIES ON RICE NOODLES

This stylish first course offers a rich and unusual contrast of tender mushrooms and refreshingly tart juicy fruit, tossed on a bed of mild rice noodles. For a variation, try using cranberries.

¼ ounce (10g) dried porcini mushrooms
5 ounces (150g) baby chestnut or button mushrooms
5 ounces (150g) oyster mushrooms
5 ounces (150g) shiitake mushrooms
2 tablespoons olive oil
4 large cloves garlic, finely sliced
1 tablespoon finely sliced ginger
6 scallions, sliced diagonally
1½ cups (350ml) vegetable stock
2 tablespoons soy sauce
8 ounces (200g) thin rice noodles
⅔ cup (100g) blueberries, defrosted if frozen

PREPARATION TIME 20 minutes, including soaking
COOKING TIME 30 minutes
SERVES 6

1 Rinse any grit off the porcini mushrooms, then leave them to soak in hot water for 20 minutes. Drain them, reserving the soaking liquid. Rinse, then dry them on paper towels and slice thinly. **2** Meanwhile, slice the baby chestnut and oyster mushrooms; remove and discard the stems from the shiitakes, then slice them. Set them all aside. **3** Heat the oil in a wok or a heavy frying pan. Add the garlic, ginger, and scallions and stir-fry for 4–5 minutes, until the garlic is nicely browned. Add all the mushrooms and continue stir-frying for 2–3 minutes. **4** Combine the reserved mushroom soaking liquid with enough stock to measure 1½ cups (400ml). Add to the mushrooms with the soy sauce. Bring the mixture to a boil, then reduce the heat and simmer, uncovered, for 20 minutes, stirring occasionally. **5** Meanwhile, put a kettle of water on to boil. Put the rice noodles in a large heatproof bowl, cover them with the boiling water, and leave them to soak for the time indicated on the package. **6** Add the blueberries to the mushrooms, increase the heat, and boil for 2–3 minutes, until the liquid has thickened slightly and the blueberries are heated through. **7** Drain the noodles, add them to the mushroom mixture in the wok, and toss together. Spoon into six serving bowls and serve while still hot.

NUTRIENTS PER SERVING CAL 177 • CARBOHYDRATE 30g (sugars 3g) • PROTEIN 4g • FAT 4g (saturated fat 1g) • FIBER 1g • SODIUM 484mg

Despite their misleading name, **sweet potatoes** are a healthy form of starch and a good source of potassium and vitamins A and C.

SPICED VEGETABLE WEDGES

For a really flavorful dish, choose a curry paste with a strong flavor.

About 1½ pounds (700g) mixed vegetables, such as celery root, parsnips, sweet potatoes, and winter squash, cut into chunks
4–5 tablespoons curry paste

TO GARNISH chopped cilantro leaves
TO SERVE low-fat Greek-style yogurt

PREPARATION TIME 10 minutes
COOKING TIME 25 minutes
SERVES 4

1 Preheat the oven to 425°F (220°C). Cook all the vegetables in boiling water: carrots and celery root for 4–5 minutes; parsnips, sweet potatoes, and squash for 3 minutes. Drain the vegetables well and put into a large bowl. **2** Stir the curry paste gently into the vegetables, until coated. **3** Spread the vegetables in a shallow baking dish and roast for about 20 minutes, or until tender. Stir once or twice during roasting to ensure even browning. **4** Sprinkle with cilantro. Serve the wedges with a bowl of yogurt for dipping.

NUTRIENTS PER SERVING CAL 140 • CARBOHYDRATE 21g (sugars 7g) • PROTEIN 3g • FAT 5g (saturated fat 1g) • FIBER 6g • SODIUM 304mg

WATERCRESS AND RICOTTA SOUFFLÉ

Grown beside streams, watercress has a robust and peppery taste, which goes well with the mild, low-fat ricotta. Serve with crusty bread and roasted tomatoes.

2 tablespoons butter
¼ cup (25g) all-purpose flour
1⅓ cups (300ml) 2 percent milk
4 eggs, separated
½ cup (150g) ricotta cheese
1 ounce (25g) aged vegetarian Cheddar
cheese, grated

½ teaspoon English mustard
Salt and black pepper
3 ounces watercress, trimmed and finely chopped

PREPARATION TIME 20 minutes
COOKING TIME 30 minutes
SERVES 6 as a starter

NUTRIENTS PER SERVING CAL 180
- **CARBOHYDRATE 6g (sugars 3g)**
- **PROTEIN 10g**
- **FAT 12g (saturated fat 6g)**
- **FIBER 0g • SODIUM 160mg**

1 Preheat the oven to 375°F (190°C). Grease six ½-cup (125ml) ramekins. **2** Melt the butter in a saucepan, stir in the flour, and cook for 1 minute. Gradually stir in the milk to make a smooth sauce. Remove the pan from the heat, cool slightly, then stir in the egg yolks, one at a time. **3** Add the ricotta, Cheddar, mustard, and salt and pepper to taste. Add the watercress, stirring well. **4** In a clean bowl, whisk the egg whites until stiff. Beat 1 tablespoon of egg whites into the sauce, then fold in the remainder, using a metal spoon. **5** Spoon the mixture into the prepared ramekins and bake for 18–20 minutes, until risen and golden. Serve at once.

Peppery dark green watercress leaves are among the healthiest of fresh salad vegetables.

SOUPS

GREEN BEAN SOUP

A trio of beans—green, fava, and flageolet—come together to add their individual flavors to this delicate pale green soup, flavored with chives.

2 tablespoons olive oil
4 cups (1l) vegetable stock
1 medium onion, chopped
1 large clove garlic
8 ounces (225g) thin green beans
12 ounces (350g) fresh frozen fava beans

15-ounce (425g) can canned flageolet or navy beans
Salt and black pepper

TO GARNISH a small bunch of chives

TOTAL TIME 30 minutes
SERVES 4–6

1 Heat the olive oil gently in a large saucepan and heat the stock in another saucepan. Add the onion and garlic to the oil and stir. **2** Trim the green beans, chop into 1-inch (2.5cm) pieces, and add them and the fava beans to the pan. Raise the heat and cook for a few minutes. **3** Add the stock to the pan and boil for 5 minutes, then lower heat and simmer for 10 minutes. **4** Remove saucepan from the heat and stir in canned flageolet beans with their liquid. Stir well. **5** Process or blend half the soup to a puree, then return it to the pan. Season to taste, then reheat. Rinse the chives and any chive flowers, snip them over the soup, and serve.

NUTRIENTS PER SERVING (4 servings) CAL 185 • CARBOHYDRATE 20g (sugars 5g)
• PROTEIN 11g • FAT 7g (saturated fat 1g) • FIBER 10g • SODIUM 346mg

Fava beans are nutritious, filling, and can be enjoyed raw. They're a great low-fat, high-fiber food and are full of minerals and vitamins.

CREAMY AVOCADO AND COCONUT SOUP

Tropical flavors of chile, coconut, and cilantro characterize this cold pureed soup, which takes its silky texture and velvety taste from luscious ripe avocados and smooth, creamy Greek yogurt.

½ vegetable boullion cube
4 scallions
1 large clove garlic
1 fresh green chile
Small bunch of cilantro
2 medium avocados
10 ounces (300g) plain Greek-style yogurt
⅔ cup (150ml) coconut milk

1 tablespoon olive oil
Pinch of sugar
½ lemon
Salt and black pepper

TOTAL TIME 15 minutes
SERVES 4

1 Dissolve the stock cube in just a little hot water in a measuring cup, then add enough cold water to make 1¼ cups (300ml). 2 Trim and chop the scallions. Peel and crush the garlic. Seed and chop the chile and set them all aside. 3 Rinse and dry the cilantro. Set aside a few leaves for a garnish and roughly chop the remainder. 4 Halve and pit the avocados and scoop the flesh into a blender or food processor. Add the stock, scallions, garlic, chile, chopped cilantro, yogurt, coconut milk, olive oil, sugar, and 1 tablespoon of juice from the lemon and process until velvety and smooth. 5 Season to taste, and chill for as long as possible. Garnish with the cilantro leaves and cracked black pepper.

NUTRIENTS PER SERVING CAL 342 • CARBOHYDRATE 8g (sugars 5g) • PROTEIN 7g • FAT 31g (saturated fat 8g) • FIBER 3g • SODIUM 202mg

HOT MOROCCAN BEAN SOUP

This filling soup is given extra heat with harissa, the fiery chile paste from North Africa.

¾ cup (200g) canned cannellini beans
2½ cups (400g) canned chickpeas
1 cup (150g) chopped onion
1 large tomato, peeled and chopped
2 tablespoons lemon juice
1 teaspoon ground cumin
1 teaspoon turmeric
2 ounces (50g) rice noodles
2 tablespoons chopped fresh cilantro

1–2 teaspoons harissa paste
Salt and black pepper

TO GARNISH sprigs of cilantro

PREPARATION TIME 10 minutes
COOKING TIME 45 minutes
SERVES 4 as a main meal, or 6 as a starter

1 Rinse and drain the beans and chickpeas and place them in a large saucepan with the onions, tomatoes, lemon juice, cumin, and turmeric. Add 7 cups (1.7l) of water. Bring to a boil, then reduce the heat, cover, and simmer for 30 minutes. **2** Stir the rice noodles into the soup and simmer for another 5 minutes. Then stir in the chopped cilantro and the harissa and add salt and pepper to taste. **3** Ladle the soup into warmed bowls, garnish with sprigs of cilantro, and serve.

NUTRIENTS PER SERVING CAL 200 • CARBOHYDRATE 35g (sugars 5g) • PROTEIN 10g
• FAT 3g (saturated fat 0.5g) • FIBER 7g • SODIUM 353mg

BORSCHT WITH CILANTRO AND CUMIN

Beets are delicious teamed with other vegetables, as in this version of the Russian classic.

1 pound (500g) raw beets, peeled and chopped
1 rib celery, chopped
2 ounces (50g) button mushrooms, sliced
1 cup (150g) chopped onion
1 small red or yellow pepper, seeded and
  chopped
1 large potato, peeled and chopped
2 tablespoons olive or sunflower oil
2 teaspoons ground cilantro
1 teaspoon cumin seeds

5 cups (1.2l) vegetable stock
Pinch of dried thyme
Salt and black pepper

TO GARNISH 4 ounces (150g) low-fat plain
  yogurt and chopped fresh chives

PREPARATION TIME 15 minutes
COOKING TIME 40 minutes
SERVES 6

1 Combine the beets, celery, mushrooms, onions, pepper, and potatoes into a large saucepan and stir in the oil. Cook over a high heat, stirring, until the vegetables start to sizzle. Cover the pan, reduce the heat to low, and simmer for 10 minutes without lifting the lid. **2** Stir in the cilantro and cumin and cook for another 1–2 minutes. Add the stock and thyme, bring to a boil, then lower the heat and simmer for 20 minutes, stirring occasionally. **3** Season with salt and pepper to taste. Pour the soup into bowls and garnish each serving with yogurt and a sprinkling of chives.

NUTRIENTS PER SERVING CAL 115 • CARBOHYDRATE 16g (sugars 10g) • PROTEIN 4g
• FAT 5g (saturated fat 1g) • FIBER 3g • SODIUM 274mg

BROCCOLI AND CAULIFLOWER CHEESE SOUP

A favorite family dish is transformed into a tasty speckled soup, perfect for a light lunch or supper.

8 ounces (250g) broccoli, broken into florets
8 ounces (250g) cauliflower, broken into florets
1 shallot, chopped
2¾ cups (600ml) vegetable stock
1⅓ cups (300ml) skim milk
¼ cup (40g) tiny pasta shapes for soup
⅔ cup (75g) low-fat aged grated Cheddar cheese

1 tablespoon chopped fresh chives
Salt and black pepper

TO GARNISH a pinch of grated nutmeg

PREPARATION TIME 10 minutes
COOKING TIME 25 minutes
SERVES 4

1 Combine the broccoli, cauliflower, shallot, and stock in a large saucepan. Bring to a boil, cover, then reduce the heat and simmer for 10 minutes, or until the florets are tender. Puree in a food processor or with a handheld mixer. **2** Return the soup to the pan and add the milk and pasta. Gently bring it to a steady simmer, then cover and cook for another 10 minutes, or until the pasta is tender. **3** Stir in the cheese and chives, reserving some chives for a garnish, and simmer for a few more minutes, stirring occasionally, until the cheese has melted and the soup has thickened slightly. Do not boil it, or the cheese will become stringy. **4** Season to taste, garnish with the reserved chives and a sprinkling of nutmeg, and serve in warmed bowls.

NUTRIENTS PER SERVING CAL 156 • CARBOHYDRATE 15g (sugars 7g) • PROTEIN 15g • FAT 5g (saturated fat 2g) • FIBER 3g • SODIUM 465mg

Unlike most other vegetables, **carrots** are more nutritious eaten cooked than raw. They are an excellent source of beta carotene, the plant form of vitamin A.

SPICY CARROT SOUP

Carrots and ginger bring out the best in each other. Here they are boosted with fresh green chile and Eastern spices in a thick vegetable soup to make a real winter warmer.

4 cups (1l) vegetable stock or water
1 small to medium potato
1 medium onion
1 pound (500g) carrots
2 large cloves garlic
Salt and black pepper
1 fresh green chile
2-inch (5cm) piece fresh ginger
1 lemon or lime

2 tablespoons olive oil
1 teaspoon garam masala or Chinese five-spice powder
1 teaspoon toasted sesame oil

TO GARNISH fresh cilantro leaves, lemon or lime zest, or croutons

TOTAL TIME 30 minutes
SERVES 4–6

1 Bring the stock to a boil in a large saucepan. Peel the potato, onion, and carrots and cut them into small chunks. Peel and quarter the garlic cloves. **2** When the stock is boiling, stir in the vegetables, garlic, and some salt. Bring it back to a boil, reduce the heat, partially cover, and boil gently for 15–20 minutes. **3** Meanwhile, seed and chop the chile, peel and chop the ginger, and squeeze the juice from the lemon. **4** Heat the olive oil in a small pan and fry the chile and ginger for about 1 minute, but do not let them burn. Stir in the garam masala and the lemon juice; cook for 1 minute. **5** Add the sesame oil and stir over the heat until the mixture thickens to form a sauce. Remove the pan from the heat and set aside. **6** When the vegetables are tender, stir in the ginger sauce, then process or blend the mixture into a smooth puree. Return the puree to the pan, season with black pepper to taste, then reheat and serve with the garnish of your choice.

NUTRIENTS PER SERVING CAL 149 • CARBOHYDRATE 19g (sugars 9g) • PROTEIN 3g • FAT 9g (saturated fat 1g) • FIBER 4g • SODIUM 330mg

ZUCCHINI AND WATERCRESS SOUP

The mellow smoothness of the zucchini in this intensely green vegetable soup provides a subtle counterbalance to the underlying sharp, peppery flavor of the watercress leaves.

2 medium onions
2 tablespoons unsalted butter
3 cups (700ml) vegetable stock
2 pounds (900g) firm zucchini, thinly sliced
1 large bunch of watercress

1 lemon
Salt and black pepper

TOTAL TIME 30 minutes
SERVES 4

1 Peel and chop the onions. Melt the butter in a large saucepan over low heat and fry the onions until they are translucent. Add the stock, cover, and bring to a boil. **2** Add the zucchini to the boiling stock. Reduce the heat, cover, and simmer for 15 minutes. **3** Rinse the watercress, discard the coarse stems, and reserve four sprigs for a garnish. Chop the remainder. **4** When the zucchini are tender, stir in the watercress, then remove the pan from the heat and leave to stand, covered, for 5 minutes. Meanwhile, squeeze the juice from the lemon and set aside. **5** Blend the soup to a puree, then add the seasoning and lemon juice to taste. Reheat and garnish with watercress.

NUTRIENTS PER SERVING CAL 119 • CARBOHYDRATE 9g (sugars 7g) • PROTEIN 6g • FAT 6g (saturated fat 4g) • FIBER 3g • SODIUM 302mg

COOL CUCUMBER SOUP

This is a great soup to make on a steamy summer's day since it requires no cooking at all. Just assemble the ingredients and mix them together. Then it is ready to eat and enjoy.

1 large cucumber
4 bushy sprigs of mint
2 cups (500g) plain yogurt
1½ cups (150ml) half-and-half
2 tablespoons white wine vinegar
Salt and black pepper

TO GARNISH 4 small sprigs of mint
TO SERVE ice cubes, optional

TOTAL TIME 15 minutes
SERVES 4

1 Chill four soup bowls in the refrigerator. Grate the cucumber coarsely, with its skin, into a large bowl. **2** Strip the leaves from the mint stems and shred enough to make 4 tablespoons, or bundle the leaves together and cut them diagonally into fine strips with kitchen scissors. Add the mint to the cucumber. **3** Stir the yogurt, half-and-half, and vinegar into the bowl. Season well with salt and pepper and stir again. **4** Divide the soup among the four chilled soup bowls. Add one or two ice cubes to each one, if you like, to chill it quickly. Garnish with the small sprigs of mint and serve.

NUTRIENTS PER SERVING CAL 182 • CARBOHYDRATE 13g (sugars 12g) • PROTEIN 9g • FAT 11g (saturated fat 7g) • FIBER 0.7g • SODIUM 114mg

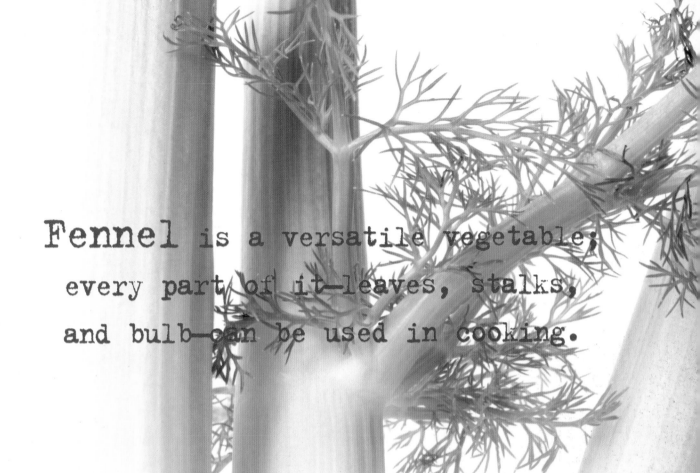

Fennel is a versatile vegetable; every part of it—leaves, stalks, and bulb—can be used in cooking.

FENNEL, PEA, AND MINT SOUP

This intensely colored soup, with just the right combination of smooth and chunky textures and herby flavors, makes a lovely light lunch, too.

1½ pounds (600g) fennel, chopped
3 cups (500g) fresh or frozen peas
4 cups (900ml) vegetable stock
3 tablespoons chopped fresh mint
Salt and black pepper

TO GARNISH a few small lettuce leaves, such as oak-leaf lettuce, and a few sprigs of fresh herbs, such as chervil and mint

PREPARATION TIME 5 minutes
COOKING TIME 25 minutes
SERVES 4–6

1 Combine the fennel, peas, and stock in a large saucepan and bring to a boil, then reduce the heat, cover, and simmer for 20 minutes, or until the fennel is tender. **2** Add the chopped mint and simmer for another minute. **3** Reserve a cupful of the vegetables and puree the remaining mixture in a food processor or with a handheld mixer. Scrape the puree back into the pan. **4** Return the reserved vegetables to the soup and reheat. Season to taste with salt and pepper, then serve, garnished with the lettuce leaves and herbs.

NUTRIENTS PER SERVING CAL 127 • CARBOHYDRATE 18g (sugars 5g) • PROTEIN 10g
• FAT 3g (saturated fat 0g) • FIBER 9g • SODIUM 312mg

MUSHROOM SOUP

The earthy flavor of the large, dark mushrooms in this soup is given a lift by garlic, parsley, and mace. It has a deep smoky color and a rich taste that needs no cream to enhance it.

5 cups (1.2l) vegetable stock
5 ounces (140g) rustic-style bread (about 5 slices)
½ small onion or 1 shallot
1½ pounds (650g) large, flat mushrooms
3 sprigs of parsley
2 tablespoons olive oil
½ small clove garlic
Pinch of ground mace or freshly grated nutmeg
Salt and black pepper

TOTAL TIME 30 minutes
SERVES 4–6

1 Put the stock on to boil. Soak the bread in a little cold water. **2** Peel and chop the onion. Clean and roughly chop the mushrooms. Chop the parsley. **3** Heat the oil in a large pan over medium heat. Fry the onion until lightly browned. Peel the garlic and crush it into the pan. Add the mushrooms and cook until they release their liquid; add the parsley. **4** Squeeze as much water as possible from the bread, then stir it into the mushrooms. Add the stock and mace. Return the soup to a boil, half cover the pan, and simmer for 15–20 minutes. **5** Puree or blend the soup until it is creamy but still slightly grainy, then reheat, season with salt and pepper, and serve.

NUTRIENTS PER SERVING CAL 161 • CARBOHYDRATE 19g (sugars 2g) • PROTEIN 6g • FAT 7g (saturated fat 1g) • FIBER 1.5g • SODIUM 400mg

AROMATIC PARSNIP SOUP

This fragrant, warming winter soup has a yogurt creaminess and subtle spicing, with a sweet undertone of apple. Serve it with hot, crusty bread for a hearty starter or light lunch.

3½ cups (850ml) vegetable stock
1 large cooking apple
1¼ pounds (550g) parsnips
1 medium onion
1 tablespoon sunflower oil
1 clove garlic
2 teaspoons ground cilantro
1 teaspoon ground cumin
1 teaspoon turmeric
Salt
1¼ cups (300ml) milk

TO GARNISH a few sprigs of cilantro and
    4–6 tablespoons plain yogurt

TOTAL TIME 30 minutes
SERVES 4–6

1 Warm the stock over low heat. Peel the apple and the parsnips. Quarter and core the apple, then chop the apple and parsnips into chunks and set aside. Peel and chop the onion. **2** Heat the oil in a large saucepan, add the onion, and leave it to soften. **3** Peel and roughly chop the garlic, add it to the pan, then add the spices and cook for 1 minute. **4** Pour the warmed stock into the pan and add the apple, parsnips, and salt. Bring to a boil, then reduce the heat, cover, and simmer for 15 minutes. **5** Meanwhile, strip off the cilantro leaves. **6** Remove the pan from the heat and stir in the milk. Process or blend the soup to a smooth puree, then reheat. **7** Ladle the soup into bowls, garnish it with the cilantro, and serve. Prepare a dish of plain low-fat yogurt to pass around separately for people to help themselves.

NUTRIENTS PER SERVING CAL 200 • **CARBOHYDRATE 22g (sugars 7g)** • **PROTEIN 6g**
• **FAT 8g (saturated fat 3g)** • **FIBER 7g** • **SODIUM 345mg**

LEMONY LENTIL SOUP

This sturdy, soothing winter soup has a delicious citrus overtone combined with the warm flavors of roasted spices. It makes an interesting change from more familiar lentil-based soups.

1 tablespoon olive oil
3 cloves garlic, coarsely chopped
1½ cups (250g) coarsely chopped onion
1¼ cups (250g) red lentils, rinsed and drained
5 cups (1.2l) vegetable stock
1 teaspoon ground cilantro
½ teaspoon ground cumin

Juice of 1 lemon
4 wafer-thin slices of lemon
Salt and black pepper

PREPARATION TIME 5 minutes
COOKING TIME 35 minutes
SERVES 4

1 Heat the oil in a heavy saucepan over medium heat. Add the garlic and onions and sauté for 6–7 minutes until they turn a rich brown color, stirring frequently to prevent them from sticking. **2** Add the lentils and cook for another 1–2 minutes. Then add the stock, raise the heat, and bring the soup to a boil. Reduce the heat, cover, and simmer for 15–20 minutes, until the lentils are almost soft. **3** Place a nonstick frying pan over high heat, add the cilantro and cumin, and dry-fry them for 1–2 minutes until the aroma rises, then add them to the soup. **4** Raise the heat under the soup, add the lemon juice and lemon slices, and season to taste, then let it simmer for 5 minutes. Sprinkle the soup with a little black pepper and serve.

NUTRIENTS PER SERVING CAL 261 • CARBOHYDRATE 40g (sugars 5g) • PROTEIN 18g • FAT 5g (saturated fat 1g) • FIBER 4g • SODIUM 310mg

WINTER PUMPKIN AND RICE SOUP

This is a hearty, warming soup, perfect for cold, damp winter days. When pureed, the pumpkin and rice give the soup a velvety texture, and a little curry powder adds a subtle touch of heat. This soup makes a tempting and filling starter.

2 pounds (1kg) pumpkin or butternut squash
2 tablespoons extra virgin olive oil
2 onions, chopped
1 teaspoon mild curry powder
2 garlic cloves, finely chopped
1 fresh hot green chile, seeded and
  finely chopped
4 cups (1l) vegetable stock, plus more as
  needed
1 cup (175g) risotto rice
Salt and black pepper
1 tablespoon chopped fresh cilantro

PREPARATION TIME 20 minutes
COOKING TIME 40–45 minutes
SERVES 6

1 Peel the pumpkin and remove the seeds and fibers from the center. Rinse the seeds and reserve. Cut the pumpkin flesh into cubes. **2** Heat the oil in a large saucepan over medium heat. Add the onions and curry powder and cook over a low to medium heat, stirring frequently, for 15–20 minutes or until the onions soften and start to caramelize. **3** Add the cubes of pumpkin, the garlic, and chile, and stir to coat with the onion mixture. Pour in the stock and add 5 tablespoons of the rice. Bring to a boil, then cover the pan, reduce the heat, and simmer for 25 minutes, or until the pumpkin and rice are very soft. **4** Meanwhile, bring a saucepan of water to a boil, add the remaining rice, and simmer for about 15 minutes or until just tender. Drain in a strainer, rinse lightly under cold water, and leave to drain again. **5** Preheat the broiler. Spread out the pumpkin seeds on a baking sheet in a single layer and toast under the broiler for 3–5 minutes, until golden and aromatic, turning them several times. Set aside. **6** When the pumpkin and rice are soft, puree the soup, either in a blender or food processor or using a handheld blender directly in the pan. **7** Stir in the cooked rice and season with salt and pepper to taste. Reheat gently. If the soup seems too thick, stir in a little hot vegetable stock or water. Stir in the chopped cilantro and serve, sprinkled with the toasted pumpkin seeds.

NUTRIENTS PER SERVING CAL 179 • CARBOHYDRATE 30g (sugars 6g) • PROTEIN 4g • FAT 5g (saturated fat 1g) • FIBER 2.5g • SODIUM 192mg

RED PEPPER AND ORANGE VELVET SOUP

A soup to delight the senses, this derives its stunning color from red peppers and its heady aroma and fruity flavor from orange flower water and freshly squeezed orange juice.

2 tablespoons olive oil
2 pounds (1kg) red bell peppers
Salt
3 oranges
1 tablespoon orange flower water

TO GARNISH orange zest, chopped fresh
    parsley, or croutons, optional

TOTAL TIME 30 minutes
SERVES 4

1 Heat the oil in a large saucepan over medium heat. Seed and quarter the peppers lengthwise. Slice them fairly coarsely in a food processor and add to the oil. Alternatively, slice them by hand, adding the first pepper to the pan while you slice the next, stirring with each addition and keeping the pan covered while you slice. Add a little salt to taste. **2** Wash any wax from the oranges, then grate the zest from one into the pan. Cover and increase the heat to high until steam starts to escape from under the lid. Lower the heat and simmer, covered, for 15–18 minutes, shaking the pan occasionally, allowing the peppers to cook in their own juice. **3** Meanwhile, squeeze the juice from the oranges into a measuring cup—you will need 3/4 cup (175ml). Stir the orange flower water into the orange juice. **4** When the peppers are soft, process or blend them to a smooth puree. It does not matter if some of the peppers have caramelized—this just adds to the flavor. Add the orange mixture and process or blend again. **5** Reheat and garnish with orange zest, herbs, and croutons, if desired.

NUTRIENTS PER SERVING CAL 130 • CARBOHYDRATE 17g (sugars 16g) • PROTEIN 2g • FAT 6g (saturated fat 1g) • FIBER 4g • SODIUM 10mg

TOMATO AND BREAD SOUP

This variation on the traditional Italian peasant soup made with day-old bread gains a wonderful flavor from garlic, herbs, and balsamic vinegar, and the bread gives it a satisfying texture.

2 tablespoons olive oil
1 cup (150g) chopped onion
1 dried red chile, seeded and chopped
2 cloves garlic, crushed
1 tablespoon chopped fresh thyme
2 pounds (1kg) tomatoes, cut into quarters
2⅔ cups (600ml) vegetable stock
Pinch of sugar
5 slices (125g) day-old white bread, cubed
2 tablespoons balsamic vinegar

2 tablespoons chopped fresh basil leaves
Salt and black pepper

TO GARNISH fresh basil leaves

PREPARATION TIME 15 minutes, plus
  10 minutes soaking time
COOKING TIME 25 minutes
SERVES 6

1 Heat 1 tablespoon of the oil in a saucepan over low heat. Add the onions, chile, garlic, and thyme, and fry for 5 minutes, or until they have softened and are lightly golden. **2** Add the tomatoes, stock, and sugar to the onions and bring them to a boil. Cover the pan, reduce the heat, and simmer for 20 minutes. **3** Meanwhile, put the bread cubes into a small bowl, add the vinegar, the remaining 1 tablespoon oil, and ¼ cup (50ml) cold water and leave them to soak for 10 minutes. **4** Puree the tomato mixture, bread, and basil together with a handheld mixer or in a food processor until very smooth. **5** Return the soup to the pan, season to taste, and reheat it gently. Pour the soup into warmed bowls, garnish with a few leaves of basil, and serve.

NUTRIENTS PER SERVING CAL 126 • CARBOHYDRATE 18g (sugars 9g) • PROTEIN 3g
• FAT 5g (saturated fat 1g) • FIBER 2g • SODIUM 320mg

FRENCH VEGETABLE SOUP

This elegant combination of fresh spring vegetables, cooked together and then added to a rich tomato-flavored broth, makes a hearty soup that will serve as a main course for lunch or supper.

2 tablespoons butter
2 cloves garlic
2 shallots
3 15-ounce cans (1.2kg) diced tomatoes
1¾ cups (400ml) vegetable stock
1 teaspoon dried basil
Salt and black pepper
8 ounces (200g) baby new potatoes
12 baby or 4 small carrots
6 large radishes
⅔ cup (100g) sugar snap peas or snowpeas, halved
12 asparagus tips
½ cup (125ml) half-and-half
8 large basil leaves

TO GARNISH aged Cheddar, optional

TOTAL TIME 30 minutes
SERVES 4

1 Put a kettle of water on to boil. Melt the butter very slowly in a large saucepan. Peel and chop the garlic and shallots, add them to the butter, and fry gently for 3 minutes, stirring occasionally. **2** Add the tomatoes and their liquid, stock, dried basil, and some salt and pepper to the pan. Cover and simmer for 15 minutes. **3** Meanwhile, scrub and quarter the potatoes, put them into a second saucepan, and cover well with the boiling water from the kettle. Bring back to a boil, then reduce the heat and boil gently. **4** Trim, scrub, and halve the baby carrots, or if you are using larger ones, peel them and cut into 1-inch (2.5cm) chunks. When the potatoes have been cooking for about 5 minutes, add the carrots. **5** Trim and rinse the radishes, then dice them and add them to the carrots and potatoes. Add the asparagus tips and the sugar snap. **6** Cook the vegetables for a total of 10–12 minutes, until they are just tender. Meanwhile, grate the cheese, if using, and set aside. **7** Drain the vegetables and add to the tomato stock. Stir in the half-and-half. Tear and add the basil leaves. **8** Season to taste with salt and pepper. Serve the soup immediately, ladling it into warmed bowls and passing the Cheddar cheese separately to sprinkle over the top, if using.

NUTRIENTS PER SERVING CAL 247 • CARBOHYDRATE 28g (sugars 4g) • PROTEIN 8g • FAT 12g (saturated fat 7g) • FIBER 6g • SODIUM 488mg • SALT 1.2g

WINTER VEGETABLE SOUP

Other winter vegetables can also be used in this thick, warming soup. Try Jerusalem artichokes or rutabagas in place of the parsnips or carrots. Accompany with garlic-flavored croutons.

1 tablespoon olive oil
2 tablespoons butter
1 large onion, chopped
½ cup (125g) sliced leeks
8 ounces (280g) parsnips, chopped
1 pound (400g) carrots, chopped
1 large potato, peeled and chopped
4 cups (900ml) vegetable stock

4–5 tablespoons 2 percent milk, optional
Salt, black pepper, and freshly grated nutmeg
2 tablespoons chopped fresh parsley

PREPARATION TIME 20 minutes
COOKING TIME 35–40 minutes
SERVES 4

1 Heat the oil and butter in a large saucepan over medium heat. Add the onion and leek and cook, stirring for 4–5 minutes until soft. Add the parsnips, carrots, and potato and cook, stirring, for 2–3 minutes. **2** Pour in the stock, bring to a boil, then simmer for 20–25 minutes, until all the vegetables are tender. **3** Transfer to a blender or food processor and process until smooth. Return to the saucepan and pour in a little milk to thin, if needed. Season with salt, pepper, and nutmeg, then stir in the parsley. **4** Reheat gently, then transfer to warmed bowls and serve.

NUTRIENTS PER SERVING CAL 215 • CARBOHYDRATE 29g (sugars 13g) • PROTEIN 5g • FAT 9g (saturated fat 4g) • FIBER 7g • SODIUM 377mg

Few foods are more nourishing than milk. It is an important source of protein and contains essential calcium, B vitamins, and zinc.

SPRING VEGETABLE SOUP WITH LEMON

This refreshing soup mixes unusual sour and sweet flavors. Serve it hot or chilled, with a glass of ice-cold vodka. Either way, it makes a delicious starter, full of the promise of summer.

1 cup (125g) cubed potatoes
1 cup (150g) chopped onion
2 stalks lemongrass, tough outer leaves removed, finely chopped
5 cups (1.2l) vegetable stock
1 cup (50g) finely shredded sorrel
1 cup (50g) finely shredded spinach
1 cup (50g) finely sliced scallions
1 fresh red chile, seeded and finely chopped

2 cloves garlic, finely sliced
1–2 tablespoons sugar or honey
Salt
3–4 tablespoons lemon juice

PREPARATION TIME 15 minutes
COOKING TIME 20–25 minutes
SERVES 4

1 Combine the potatoes, onions, lemongrass, and stock in a large heavy saucepan and bring it all to a boil. Reduce the heat, cover, and simmer for 15–20 minutes, until the potatoes are just cooked. 2 Stir in the sorrel, spinach, scallions, chile, garlic, sugar, and a pinch of salt. Bring the soup to a boil and cook for 1 minute. 3 Remove the soup from the heat and add lemon juice to taste. Serve it hot or chilled.

NUTRIENTS PER SERVING CAL 59 • CARBOHYDRATE 10g (sugars 7g) • PROTEIN 4g
• FAT 1g (saturated fat 0g) • FIBER 2g • SODIUM 326mg

GAZPACHO

This crunchy, floating salad, one of many versions of the celebrated Spanish soup, is incomparable on a hot day. The combination of textures and flavors is really satisfying.

1 thick slice dry-textured bread
6 tablespoons extra virgin olive oil
4 tablespoons red wine vinegar
Salt and black pepper
1 tablespoon paprika, or hot or sweet Spanish paprika (pimenton)
2½ cups (600g) canned chopped tomatoes in natural juice
1 red onion
4 large cloves garlic
1 large cucumber
1 each, red, yellow, and green bell peppers
1 fresh or dried red chile, or 1 fresh green chile
6 large basil and/or mint leaves
1⅓ cups (300ml) ice-cold water
12 ice cubes, optional

TO GARNISH 1 clove garlic, a little olive oil, and 3 slices of bread for croutons, optional

TIME 30 minutes
SERVES 4–6

1 Discard the crust from the bread, then put it into a food processor and make it into crumbs. 2 Put the oil into a large serving bowl and whisk in the vinegar and salt to make a creamy emulsion. Add the paprika and the bread crumbs and stir until thoroughly combined and sloppy. 3 Stir the tomatoes and their juice into the mixture, then set it aside. 4 Peel the onion, garlic, and cucumber. Halve and seed the peppers and the chile, then cut them into quarters. 5 In a food processor, coarsely chop the onion and garlic together and add them to the bread crumb mixture. One by one, coarsely chop the cucumber, peppers, and chile and add them to the soup. 6 Rinse, dry and tear the basil or mint leaves into small pieces and add them. Stir well, taste, and season generously with salt and black pepper. The flavor should be sharp and refreshing, with plenty of bite. 7 Stir in enough ice-cold water to give the mixture a souplike consistency, but do not make it too thin—the texture should be quite dense. Leave to chill, or stir in the ice cubes and serve immediately. 8 To make croutons, put the garlic into a frying pan with a little oil over medium heat. Cut the bread into cubes and fry, turning often, until browned. Discard the garlic; serve the croutons with the soup if desired.

NUTRIENTS PER SERVING CAL 261 • CARBOHYDRATE 21g (sugars 13g) • PROTEIN 6g • FAT 18g (saturated fat 3g) • FIBER 3g • SODIUM 118mg

VEGETABLE SOUP WITH FRAGRANT PESTO

This soup is based on pistou, the classic Provençale soup. Laden with vegetables and pasta and flavored with pesto, it makes a fabulous change from minestrone, its Italian counterpart. French bread is the traditional accompaniment, plus a glass of wine.

1 tablespoon extra virgin olive oil
1 leek, thinly sliced
1 large zucchini, diced
5 ounces (150g) thin green beans, cut into short lengths
2 garlic cloves, crushed
5½ cups (1.3l) vegetable stock
8 ounces (250g) tomatoes, chopped
Black pepper
½ cup (85g) vermicelli, broken into small pieces
2 tablespoons pesto sauce

TO SERVE 4 tablespoons freshly grated Italian-style premium cheese, such as Parmigiano Reggiano, optional

PREPARATION TIME 10 minutes
COOKING TIME about 30 minutes
SERVES 4

1 Heat the oil in a large saucepan over medium-high heat. Add the leek, zucchini, beans, and garlic and sauté for about 5 minutes, or until the vegetables are softened and beginning to turn brown. **2** Pour in the vegetable stock. Stir in the tomatoes and add freshly ground black pepper to taste. Bring to a boil, then reduce the heat and cover the pan. Simmer over low heat for 10 minutes or until the vegetables are tender but still holding their shape. **3** Stir in the vermicelli. Cover the pan again and simmer for another 5 minutes, or until the pasta is al dente. **4** Ladle the soup into bowls and add 1½ teaspoons pesto to each. Stir, then serve, offering the grated cheese separately to stir into the soup.

NUTRIENTS PER SERVING CAL 240 • CARBOHYDRATE 20.5g (sugars 4g) • PROTEIN 12g • FAT 12g (saturated fat 4.5g) • FIBER 3g • SODIUM 416mg

lads

SALADS

TROPICAL SALAD WITH LIME DRESSING

Two favorite tropical fruits—rich, creamy-smooth avocado and sweet-flavored papaya—are combined with watercress and a fresh lime dressing to make a light and stylish starter.

FOR THE DRESSING
1 lime
Salt and black pepper
¼ teaspoon sugar
4 tablespoons extra virgin olive oil
4 tablespoons sunflower oil

FOR THE SALAD
1 bunch of watercress
2 ripe, firm avocados
2 ripe, firm papayas

TOTAL TIME 20 minutes
SERVES 4

1 First make the dressing. Wash any wax from the lime and remove the zest with a zester, or grate it finely. Squeeze out 2 tablespoons of lime juice and put it with the zest in a mixing bowl. Add salt, black pepper, and the sugar, then whisk in the oils. Taste and add more lime juice, if necessary, then put the dressing aside. **2** Trim the coarse stems from the watercress. **3** Halve and pit the avocados, then peel and slice them widthwise. Halve the papayas, then remove the seeds, and peel and slice the flesh lengthwise. **4** Arrange the watercress, avocados, and papayas on individual serving plates. Pour the dressing over and serve immediately. For a variation, you can use mangoes instead of the papayas and baby spinach leaves in place of the watercress.

NUTRIENTS PER SERVING CAL 367 • CARBOHYDRATE 6g (sugars 1g) • PROTEIN 3g • FAT 36g (saturated fat 6g) • FIBER 4g • SODIUM 28mg

CUCUMBER, RADISH, AND MELON SALAD

A wonderful combination of fruit, vegetables, and crunchy almonds mixed with a honey and walnut oil dressing, this salad adds a touch of glamour and color to any meal.

1 pound (500g) watermelon or honeydew melon
1 cup (100g) diced cucumber
Salt
Olive oil for frying
¼ cup (25g) flaked almonds
¾ cup (100g) fresh bean sprouts
4 ounces (150g) radishes
4 scallions
1 small bunch of watercress

FOR THE DRESSING
1½ teaspoons honey
3 tablespoons walnut oil
1 tablespoon cider vinegar
Black pepper

TOTAL TIME 20 minutes
SERVES 4

1 Seed and dice the melon. Combine the melon and cucumber in a colander, add a little salt, and toss them together. Place a saucer on top and leave to drain. **2** Heat a little oil in a frying pan and fry the almonds until golden, then drain on paper towels. **3** Rinse the bean sprouts and drain them well. Trim the radishes and scallions. Quarter the radishes, slice the scallions, and mix all three together in a salad bowl. **4** Whisk the dressing ingredients together and pour over the salad. **5** Trim the watercress and arrange it in a shallow serving dish. Add the melon and cucumber to the salad bowl, toss the salad gently, then spoon it onto the watercress. Scatter the almonds over the top to serve.

NUTRIENTS PER SERVING CAL 231 • **CARBOHYDRATE** 15g (sugars 14g) • **PROTEIN** 4g • **FAT** 18g (saturated fat 2g) • **FIBER** 2.5g • **SODIUM** 21mg

WATERCRESS, KIWI, MUSHROOM, AND TOMATO SALAD

Serve this flavor-packed salad as a vibrant first course or as an accompaniment to a main dish.

4 ounces (125g) watercress sprigs
2 kiwifruit, peeled and thinly sliced
4 ounces (125g) button or chestnut
   mushrooms, thinly sliced
8 ounces (250g) tomatoes, sliced

FOR THE DRESSING
1 teaspoon red wine vinegar
Salt and black pepper
4 teaspoons olive oil

PREPARATION TIME 20 minutes
SERVES 4

1 Arrange a bed of watercress in a bowl, then scatter the kiwifruit, mushrooms, and tomatoes on top. **2** To make the dressing, pour the vinegar into a small bowl, season to taste, and whisk thoroughly to dissolve the salt. Add the oil and whisk again. **3** Just before serving, pour the dressing over the salad, taking care not to disturb the arrangement.

NUTRIENTS PER SERVING CAL 64 • CARBOHYDRATE 5g (sugars 5g) • PROTEIN 2g • FAT 4g (saturated fat 1g) • FIBER 2g • SODIUM 24mg

QUINOA SALAD WITH DRIED FRUIT

High in protein and low in fat, quinoa absorbs flavors well and makes a substantial salad.

1 cup (180g) quinoa grains
Salt and black pepper
2 tablespoons pine nuts
1 rib celery, finely diced
⅓ cup (50g) finely diced red onion
½ yellow bell pepper, finely diced
12 dried cranberries, snipped into pieces
⅓ cup (50g) dried currants

FOR THE DRESSING
½–1 teaspoon ground coriander

½–1 teaspoon ground cumin
1 tablespoon lemon juice
½ teaspoon paprika
1 tablespoon chopped fresh parsley

TO GARNISH fresh flat-leaved parsley

PREPARATION TIME 15 minutes
COOKING TIME 20 minutes
SERVES 4

1 Put a kettle on to boil. Put the quinoa into a large sieve and rinse it thoroughly several times in cold running water to remove its bitter flavor. **2** Put the quinoa in a saucepan with 2⅓ cups (500ml) boiling water and a pinch of salt and return to a boil. Cover, reduce the heat, and simmer for 15 minutes, or until the grains are tender but not mushy. Strain over a large bowl to catch the cooking liquid, then set both aside. **3** Toast the pine nuts in a dry frying pan for 1–2 minutes, until they are golden brown. Transfer the quinoa to a large bowl and stir in the celery, onion, bell pepper, cranberries, currants, and pine nuts. **4** To make the dressing, mix together the coriander, cumin, lemon juice, paprika, and parsley. Add up to 4 tablespoons of the quinoa cooking liquid until you have the desired sharpness. Season to taste, then stir it into the salad. Serve, garnished with parsley.

NUTRIENTS PER SERVING CAL 241 • CARBOHYDRATE 37g (sugars 14g) • PROTEIN 8g • FAT 8g (saturated fat 1g) • FIBER 1g • SODIUM 35mg

FRUITY BRUSSELS SPROUTS

Winter vegetables, served raw, make a wonderfully fresh, crunchy, and nutritious salad.

FOR THE DRESSING
1 tablespoon low-fat crème fraîche
2 tablespoons reduced-calorie mayonnaise
2 teaspoons olive oil
Grated zest and juice of 1 orange
2 teaspoons white wine vinegar
Salt and black pepper

FOR THE SALAD
8 ounces (225g) Brussels sprouts
1 sweet apple
1 cup (125g) grated carrot
3 celery sticks, chopped
2 tablespoons chopped fresh cilantro
3/4 cup (125g) pitted and chopped dates

PREPARATION TIME 25 minutes
SERVES 4

1 To make the dressing, whisk together the crème fraîche, mayonnaise, oil, orange zest and juice, and vinegar. Season to taste, and set aside. **2** Trim off and discard the bases and outer leaves of the Brussels sprouts, then shred them finely and put them in a large bowl. Cut the apple into quarters without peeling it, remove the core, then chop into small chunks and add to the bowl with the carrot and celery. **3** Stir in enough dressing to coat the salad, saving any left over to serve on the side. Scatter the cilantro and dates over the salad and serve.

NUTRIENTS PER SERVING CAL 172 • CARBOHYDRATE 30g (sugars 29g) • PROTEIN 4g
• FAT 5g (saturated fat 1g) • FIBER 5g • SODIUM 101mg

For the best results, choose firm, bright green Brussels sprouts with tightly packed leaves and no patches of yellow.

CARROT AND GINGER SALAD

This simple salad, with its surprising citrus dressing sharpened with ginger and sweetened with honey, makes a colorful—and healthy—contribution to any meal.

1 cup (140g) golden raisins
1 pound (400g) young carrots
Salt
½ teaspoon honey or sugar
½ cup (50g) chopped peanuts, pecans, or walnuts

FOR THE DRESSING
2-inch (5cm) piece fresh ginger
1 lemon
1 orange
1 cup (225ml) sour cream or plain yogurt

TOTAL TIME 30 minutes
SERVES 4

1 Put a little water into a kettle and put it on to boil. Put the golden raisins into a small bowl, cover them with the boiling water, and set them aside. **2** To make the citrus dressing, peel and finely grate the ginger into a small mixing bowl. **3** Wash any wax off the lemon and orange, then finely grate half the zest from each into the bowl. Squeeze the juice from half of each of them and add it to the ginger in the mixing bowl. Stir in the sour cream and set the dressing aside. **4** Peel the carrots and grate them into a serving bowl. Drain the raisins and add them. **5** Stir the dressing into the carrot and raisin mixture, season with salt, and add honey to taste. Finally, stir in the chopped nuts and serve.

NUTRIENTS PER SERVING CAL 315 • **CARBOHYDRATE 35g (sugars 33g)** • **PROTEIN 7g** • **FAT 18g (saturated fat 8g)** • **FIBER 4.5g** • **SODIUM 57mg**

SPINACH AND BABY CORN SALAD

Succulent morsels of rich avocado are strewn throughout this pretty combination of dark, tender spinach and arugula leaves tossed with tiny cobs of crunchy baby corn.

FOR THE DRESSING
1 avocado
1 clove garlic
3 tablespoons extra virgin olive oil
1 tablespoon white wine vinegar
1 teaspoon sugar
1 teaspoon Tabasco sauce
Salt

FOR THE SALAD
¾ cup (100g) chopped canned baby corn
1½ cups (85g) arugula leaves
4 cups (225g) baby spinach leaves

TOTAL TIME 15 minutes
SERVES 4

1 Make the dressing. Cut the avocado in half, remove the pit, and use a spoon to scoop the flesh into a large salad bowl. **2** Crush the garlic in the bowl, then add the oil, vinegar, sugar, and Tabasco sauce. Season to taste with salt, then stir the dressing together; some of the avocado will merge into the oil, but some small chunks should be present. **3** Add the baby corn, arugula, and spinach leaves to the dressing, toss well, and serve.

NUTRIENTS PER SERVING CAL 174 • CARBOHYDRATE 8g (sugars 3g) • PROTEIN 3g
• FAT 15g (saturated fat 3g) • FIBER 3g • SODIUM 96mg

BEETS WITH HORSERADISH CREAM DRESSING

With a vibrant, deep ruby-red color and a fresh flavor and texture, raw beets taste completely different from beets pickled in vinegar. They make a spectacular salad.

1½ pounds (675g) raw beets, peeled
1 small red onion, finely chopped
1 tablespoon sunflower oil
2 tablespoons orange juice
2 teaspoons red wine vinegar
Salt and black pepper
6 ounces (150g) baby salad greens, such as beet tops, baby chard, lamb's lettuce, red mustard, mizuna, baby spinach, or sorrel

HORSERADISH DRESSING
3 tablespoons sour cream
3 tablespoons plain low-fat yogurt
1 teaspoon grated fresh horseradish or 2 teaspoons horseradish sauce
2 tablespoons chopped fresh dill

PREPARATION TIME 20 minutes, plus 30 minutes marinating
SERVES 4

1 Grate the beets into a mixing bowl, keeping all the juices (this can also be done in a food processor with a coarse grating disk). Add the onion and stir to mix with the beets. **2** Whisk together the oil, orange juice, and vinegar in a small bowl. Season with salt and pepper to taste. Pour it over the beets and onion and toss well. Cover and leave to marinate at room temperature for 30 minutes. (The salad can be prepared up to this stage and kept for up to 24 hours in the refrigerator.) **3** Put the salad greens in a serving bowl. Add the marinated beets and onion and toss together. **4** For the dressing, stir the sour cream, yogurt, horseradish, and dill together. Spoon the dressing on the salad and serve immediately.

NUTRIENTS PER SERVING CAL 181 • CARBOHYDRATE 18g (sugars 16g) • PROTEIN 5g • FAT 10g (saturated fat 3g) • FIBER 4g • SODIUM 148mg

Eating onions, whether cooked or raw, may help to reduce blood cholesterol by increasing levels of the lipoproteins that help carry cholesterol away from body tissues.

Leeks are a useful
source of potassium. They help
to encourage the efficient
functioning of the kidneys and
are an effective diuretic.

MARINATED LEEKS

Enjoy this simple salad with its herb and mustard dressing as a light first course or tasty side dish.

8 slim young leeks
Salt and black pepper

FOR THE MARINADE
2 tablespoons extra virgin olive oil
2 teaspoons white wine vinegar
1 tablespoon whole-grain mustard
2 tablespoons finely chopped fresh chives
2 tablespoons finely chopped fresh parsley
1 teaspoon finely chopped fresh tarragon

TO GARNISH 4 sprigs of tarragon

TO SERVE whole-grain bread slices, optional

PREPARATION TIME 20 minutes, plus
  30 minutes marinating
COOKING TIME 10 minutes
SERVES 4

1 Bring a wide pan of salted water to a boil. Cut the leeks lengthwise or, for a dinner party presentation, cut a cross from the top of each leek through the leaves to halfway down the white part of the stem. Rinse the cut leeks in lots of cold water to remove any grit. **2** Drop half the leeks into the boiling water and boil them for 4–5 minutes, until tender. Remove with a slotted spoon and cool them under cold water. Drain and pat them dry, then arrange them in a shallow dish. Repeat with the remaining leeks. **3** Meanwhile, to make the marinade, whisk together the oil, vinegar, mustard, and herbs and season to taste. Spoon the mixture over the leeks, then use your hands to turn them so that they are well coated. Cover and leave to marinate at room temperature for 30 minutes, turning occasionally. **4** If serving as a starter, divide the leeks among four plates, fan out the leaves if cut crossways, and garnish with tarragon.

NUTRIENTS PER SERVING CAL 81 • CARBOHYDRATE 3g (sugars 3g) • PROTEIN 2g • FAT 6g (saturated fat 1g) • FIBER 4g • SODIUM 4mg

CARROT-AND-RADISH RICE SALAD WITH TOFU DRESSING

Brown rice tossed with crisp vegetables and fresh and dried fruit makes an unusual side salad. The almost fat-free dressing is based on tofu, which gives it a grainy texture similar to hummus. For a smoother, mayonnaise-like texture, use silken tofu.

1 cup (200g) long-grain brown rice
¾ cup (125g) sliced radishes
1 large carrot, cut into matchsticks
2 scallions, chopped
1 Asian pear, peeled, cored, and diced
6 tablespoons raisins
4 tablespoons coarsely chopped fresh cilantro

TOFU DRESSING
4 ounces (125g) silken tofu, diced

2 teaspoons Dijon mustard
1 tablespoon white wine vinegar
1 garlic clove, crushed
3 tablespoons orange juice
Salt and black pepper

PREPARATION AND COOKING TIME 50 minutes,
   plus cooling
SERVES 4

1 Put the rice in a saucepan, add 2⅔ cups (600ml) water, and bring to a boil. Cover and simmer very gently for 30–40 minutes, until the rice is tender and has absorbed all the water. Remove from the heat and leave to cool. **2** While the rice is cooling, make the dressing. Put the tofu in a blender or food processor and add the mustard, vinegar, garlic, and orange juice. Blend until smooth. Season with salt and pepper to taste. **3** Pour the tofu dressing into a large bowl. Add the radishes, carrot, scallions, Asian pear, raisins, and cilantro, and stir until well combined. Stir in the rice. Serve at room temperature or lightly chilled.

NUTRIENTS PER SERVING CAL 277 • CARBOHYDRATE 58g (sugars 17g) • PROTEIN 7g • FAT 3g (saturated fat 0.5g) • FIBER 3g • SODIUM 22mg

RATATOUILLE, CHINESE-STYLE

This vegetable salad is given a piquant flavor with Chinese black bean and hoisin sauces.

FOR THE DRESSING
1 tablespoon black bean sauce
1 tablespoon hoisin sauce
2 tablespoons dry sherry
A few drops of Tabasco sauce
1 teaspoon red or white wine vinegar

FOR THE SALAD
4 ounces (125g) zucchini
4 ounces (125g) eggplant
4 ounces (125g) small chestnut, oyster, or shiitake mushrooms
4 ounces (125g) tomatoes, peeled, seeded and diced
4 ounces (125g) canned water chestnuts, drained and sliced

PREPARATION TIME 25 minutes, plus 20 minutes marinating
COOKING TIME 8 minutes
SERVES 2 as a main course, 4 as a side dish

1 Put a kettle on to boil. To make the dressing, put all the ingredients into a bowl, mix together, and set aside. **2** Preheat the broiler. Cut the zucchini in half lengthwise and then into ¾-inch (2cm) chunks. Blanch them in boiling water for 2 minutes, then drain and refresh them under running cold water. Dry them on paper towels. **3** Cut the eggplant into ½-inch (1cm) slices. Broil the slices on a baking sheet for 3 minutes on each side or until they are tender. Leave them to cool, then cut them into quarters. **4** Broil the mushrooms for 5 minutes, turning occasionally, then set them aside to cool. **5** Put the vegetables into a serving dish and add the tomatoes and water chestnuts. Pour the dressing over them, mix well, and set aside to marinate for 20 minutes for the flavors to blend (do not refrigerate). **6** As a salad, serve the ratatouille at room temperature. As a side dish, pour the dressed salad into a hot nonstick wok or frying pan and stir-fry over a high heat for 5–8 minutes, until steaming hot. Serve as a part of a vegetarian meal.

NUTRIENTS PER SERVING CAL 91 • CARBOHYDRATE 12g (sugars 8g) • PROTEIN 5g • FAT 1g (saturated fat 1g) • FIBER 4g • SODIUM 520mg

ROASTED POTATO SALAD WITH CUMIN AND YOGURT DRESSING

This hot potato salad is served with a lightly spiced, cool dressing—for a refreshing difference.

1 tablespoon olive oil
Salt
5 small baking potatoes, scrubbed
4 ounces (125g) mixed salad greens

FOR THE DRESSING
½ teaspoon ground cumin

Juice of ½ lemon
½ cup (100g) low-fat Greek yogurt
Salt and black pepper

PREPARATION TIME 15 minutes
COOKING TIME 50–55 minutes
SERVES 4

1 Preheat the oven to 400°F (200°C). In a bowl, stir together the oil and ½ teaspoon salt, then use your hands to turn and coat the potatoes in the mixture. Place the potatoes on a baking sheet and roast for 50–55 minutes, until soft when squeezed and crisp on the outside. **2** To make the dressing, place the cumin in a small ovenproof dish, such as a ramekin, and toast it in the hot oven for no more than 2 minutes while the potatoes are roasting. Do not let it burn. Remove it from the oven and leave it to cool. **3** In a small bowl, stir together the cooled cumin, lemon juice, and yogurt and add salt and pepper to taste. Cover and chill, or set aside in a cool room.
4 Arrange the salad greens on four serving plates. When the potatoes are done, remove them from the oven and, using an oven mitt for protection, quarter them lengthwise into wedges.
5 Put five potato wedges on each plate. Drizzle the warm potatoes with the dressing and serve.

NUTRIENTS PER SERVING CAL 189 • CARBOHYDRATE 32g (sugars 3g) • PROTEIN 5g
• FAT 5g (saturated fat 2g) • FIBER 3.5g • SODIUM 21mg

GRILLED VEGETABLE SALAD

Succulent vegetable juices and sherry vinegar moisten this salad so that you do not need an oily dressing. It is best made the day before, to allow the flavors to develop fully.

12 ounces (350g) eggplant
1½ pounds (700g) zucchini
Salt and black pepper
1 large red bell pepper, cut into quarters
2 tablespoons olive oil

FOR THE DRESSING
Pinch of cayenne pepper

2 cloves garlic, crushed
1 tablespoon sherry vinegar

TO GARNISH chopped fresh parsley

PREPARATION TIME 15 minutes, plus at least
  3 hours standing
COOKING TIME 20–35 minutes
SERVES 4

1 Line two baking sheets with paper towels. Cut the eggplant and zucchini lengthwise into 3/4-inch (2cm)-thick slices, put them on the sheets in a single layer, and sprinkle with salt. Set aside for 15 minutes. **2** Meanwhile, make the dressing. Mix the cayenne, garlic, and vinegar together, season to taste, and set aside. **3** Heat a ridged cast-iron grill pan over a medium-high heat or preheat the broiler. Brush the skin side of the pepper with oil and cook the pieces, skin side down on the grill pan or skin side up under the broiler, for 5 minutes, or until the pepper has softened and the skin has blackened a little. **4** Place the pepper in a large bowl, sprinkle over one-third of the dressing, and stir. **5** Rinse the eggplant and zucchini slices and pat them dry, then brush them lightly with oil. Grill for 3–4 minutes on each side for the eggplant and 2–3 minutes on each side for the zucchini. (You will need to cook them in batches if you are using a ridged grill pan.) **6** Cut the grilled eggplant and zucchini slices in half widthwise and add them to the pepper. Pour on the remaining dressing and mix well. **7** Cover and refrigerate for at least 3 hours, or overnight. Serve at room temperature.

NUTRIENTS PER SERVING CAL 106 • CARBOHYDRATE 8g (sugars 7g) • PROTEIN 4g
• FAT 7g (saturated fat 1g) • FIBER 4g • SODIUM 35mg

CHINESE-STYLE HOT NOODLE SALAD WITH VEGETABLES

Fragrant ginger and lemongrass flavor this hearty vegetable and noodle salad.

4 ounces (100g) thin egg noodles
2 teaspoons sunflower oil
1 fresh red chile, seeded and finely chopped
2–3 cloves garlic, chopped
2 tablespoons finely grated ginger
1 tablespoon finely chopped lemongrass
6 ounces (200g) carrots, cut into matchsticks
1 red bell pepper, diced
1 yellow bell pepper, diced
1 cup (150g) canned baby corn, cut in half
 lengthwise
4 ounces (100g) sugar snap peas or snow peas
2 cups (250g) finely shredded Chinese cabbage
6 scallions, finely sliced
4 tablespoons soy sauce
1 teaspoon Asian sesame oil
3 tablespoons fresh cilantro leaves
3 tablespoons salted peanuts, finely chopped

PREPARATION TIME 30 minutes
COOKING TIME 10 minutes
SERVES 4

1 Bring a large pot of salted water to a boil. Cook the noodles in boiling water according to the instructions, then drain them well. **2** Heat the sunflower oil in a hot wok or large frying pan and stir-fry the chile, garlic, ginger, lemongrass, carrots, bell peppers, baby corn, and sugar snap peas for 4–5 minutes. **3** Add the Chinese cabbage, scallions, drained noodles, soy sauce, and sesame oil. Toss everything together over a medium heat for another minute, until they are thoroughly combined and hot. **4** Finally, add the cilantro and peanuts, toss together once more, and serve.

NUTRIENTS PER SERVING CAL 236 • CARBOHYDRATE 36g (sugars 14g) • PROTEIN 9g
• FAT 9g (saturated fat 2g) • FIBER 5g • SODIUM 1180mg

WILD RICE AND FENNEL SALAD

Grapes, orange, and a handful of raisins add sweetness to a salad brimming with the earthy flavors of wild rice, chopped hazelnuts, and a nut oil, herb, and white wine vinegar dressing.

1 cup (175g) packaged long-grain and wild
   rice mixture
Salt
8 ounces (250g) cucumber
8 ounces (250g) bulb fennel
6 scallions
4 ounces (125g) seedless red grapes
½ cup (50g) skinned hazelnuts
3 tablespoons raisins
1 orange

FOR THE DRESSING
3 sprigs of chervil
2 sprigs each of tarragon and parsley
6 tablespoons hazelnut or walnut oil
1 tablespoon white wine vinegar
Salt and black pepper

TO GARNISH 4–6 sprigs of tarragon

TIME 30 minutes
SERVES 4–6

1 Bring 2 cups (425ml) water to a boil, add the rice mix and a little salt, cover, and simmer for 18–20 minutes, or until the rice is cooked and all the water absorbed. **2** Meanwhile, finely dice the cucumber; trim and thinly slice the fennel and scallions and halve the grapes. Put them all into a salad bowl. Chop the hazelnuts and add them, with the raisins. **3** Wash any wax from the orange and grate the zest into the salad. **4** To make the herb dressing, squeeze 3 tablespoons of juice from the orange and pour it into a small bowl. Finely chop the herbs and add them to the juice with the oil and vinegar. Whisk together, then season to taste. **5** Drain the cooked rice and rinse it briefly under cold running water. Drain well, mix it into the salad vegetables, and pour the dressing over. Garnish with sprigs of tarragon.

NUTRIENTS PER SERVING CAL 459 • CARBOHYDRATE 50g (sugars 12g) • PROTEIN 7g • FAT 26g (saturated fat 2g) • FIBER 4g • SODIUM 17mg

Nuts can supply many of the
nutrients that may be missing from
a vegetarian diet. Walnuts may
help to reduce the risk of
coronary heart disease.

ENDIVE, STILTON, AND WALNUT SALAD

Broiling adds a lovely smoky flavor to the endive in a nutritious salad that includes the classic British duo of Stilton and heart-healthy walnuts. Serve warm for a sophisticated comfort food.

4 small or 2 large Belgian endive heads,
  halved lengthwise and cores removed
Vegetable oil for brushing
1 large pear, peeled, cored, and sliced
2 tablespoons walnut oil
Salt and black pepper

4 ounces (100g) Stilton cheese, finely
  crumbled
3 tablespoons walnut halves, lightly toasted

PREPARATION TIME 5 minutes
COOKING TIME 8–13 minutes
SERVES 4

1 Preheat the broiler. Brush the endives lightly with vegetable oil and place on the broiler rack, cut side up. Broil them as near to the heat as possible for 2–3 minutes for smaller heads (3–4 minutes for larger heads) until beginning to soften and char. Turn, then brush lightly with oil, and continue to cook for 2–3 minutes (or 3–4 minutes) until softened and lightly charred.
2 Turn the endives over again to cut side up. Lay the pear slices on the endives, brush lightly with walnut oil, sprinkle with salt and pepper, and return to the broiler for 4–5 minutes to warm the pears. **3** Transfer to warmed plates, sprinkle with the Stilton and toasted walnuts, and drizzle with the remaining walnut oil. Serve at once.

NUTRIENTS PER SERVING CAL 235 • CARBOHYDRATE 4g (sugars 3g) • PROTEIN 7g • FAT 21g (saturated fat 7g) • FIBER 1g • SODIUM 199mg

RUSSIAN BEAN SALAD

Beets, soybeans, and potatoes are tossed in a piquant sour cream dressing, then served on a salad of arugula, fennel, and tomatoes in this delicious and refreshing main-course salad. Serve with dark rye bread so you can mop up all the creamy dressing.

1 cup (150g) dried soybeans, soaked overnight
1 pound (450g) small new potatoes, scrubbed and halved
2 large shallots, thinly sliced
1½ cups (250g) cooked beets (not pickled), peeled and diced
1 pound (500g) tomatoes, sliced
1 bulb fennel, thinly sliced
2 ounces (55g) arugula
Salt and black pepper

SOUR CREAM DRESSING
⅔ cup (150ml) sour cream
⅔ cup (150g) plain low-fat yogurt
4 gherkins, finely chopped
2 tablespoons creamed horseradish
1 teaspoon superfine sugar

PREPARATION AND COOKING TIME 3¼ hours, plus cooling
SERVES 4

1 Drain the soaked beans and rinse under cold running water. Transfer to a saucepan and cover with fresh water. Bring to a boil and boil rapidly for 10–15 minutes. Then partly cover and simmer for about 2½ hours, or until tender. Drain and leave to cool. **2** Put the potatoes into a saucepan of boiling water and simmer for about 15 minutes, or until just tender. Drain and leave until cool enough to handle. **3** Meanwhile, for the dressing, mix together the sour cream and yogurt in a large mixing bowl. Stir in the chopped gherkins, horseradish, sugar, and salt and pepper to taste. **4** Add the soybeans and shallots to the bowl and stir into the dressing. Cut the warm potatoes into cubes and add to the bean mixture, then gently fold in the beets. **5** Divide the tomatoes, fennel, and arugula among four serving plates. Spoon the soybean salad on top and serve immediately.

NUTRIENTS PER SERVING CAL 386 • CARBOHYDRATE 41g (sugars 20g) • PROTEIN 21g • FAT 16g (saturated fat 6g) • FIBER 11g • SODIUM 206mg

WARM FLAGEOLET AND CHARRED VEGETABLE SALAD

Balsamic vinegar enhances the strong flavors of the vegetables in this warm piquant salad, excellent served as a light lunch. To vary the flavor, use a good wine or cider vinegar instead.

1 red bell pepper
1 yellow bell pepper
1 medium onion
2 medium zucchini
2 tablespoons olive oil
2 large sprigs of basil
2 medium tomatoes
2¼ cups (420g) cooked flageolet or navy beans
2¼ cups (420g) cooked lentils
2 tablespoons crushed sun-dried tomatoes
   in oil
1 tablespoon balsamic vinegar
Salt and black pepper

TO GARNISH 12 large black olives

TOTAL TIME 20 minutes
SERVES 4

1 Seed and roughly chop the bell peppers. Slice the onion. Trim and thinly slice the zucchini.
2 Heat the oil in a large frying pan and sauté the peppers, onion, and zucchini over a high heat, stirring occasionally. **3** Tear the basil leaves and roughly chop the fresh tomatoes. **4** Add the beans and lentils to the pan, stir gently, then add the basil, the fresh tomatoes, the sun-dried tomatoes, and the vinegar. **5** Season the mixture, then let it heat through, stirring well. **6** Turn the salad into a warm dish, garnish with the olives, and serve immediately.

NUTRIENTS PER SERVING CAL 390 • CARBOHYDRATE 52g (sugars 9g) • PROTEIN 21g • FAT 11g (saturated fat 1g) • FIBER 12g • SODIUM 402mg

BROILED GOAT CHEESE SALAD

Crisp toasted French bread is spread with a rich red onion marmalade flavored with balsamic vinegar and rosemary, topped with creamy goat cheese and finished under the broiler. Served with a beet, pepper, and lamb's lettuce salad, it makes an impressive starter or snack lunch.

1 tablespoon extra virgin olive oil
4 small red onions, about 10 ounces (300g)
in total, thinly sliced
2 garlic cloves, finely chopped
1 teaspoon sugar
2 teaspoons balsamic vinegar
4 slices French bread
A few sprigs of rosemary
8 ounces (200g) fresh goat cheese, cut
into 4 slices
Black pepper
3 ounces (85g) lamb's lettuce

2 medium cooked beets, peeled and cut into
thin strips
1 small red bell pepper, seeded and cut into
thin strips

FOR THE DRESSING
2 tablespoons extra virgin olive oil
2 teaspoons balsamic vinegar
Salt and black pepper

PREPARATION TIME 25 minutes
SERVES 4

1 Preheat the broiler. Heat the oil in a frying pan, add the onions, and sauté for 5 minutes, stirring occasionally, until softened. Add the garlic and sugar and cook for another 5–8 minutes, stirring frequently, until the onions are very soft, browned, and caramelized. Stir in the balsamic vinegar. **2** Lightly toast the French bread on both sides under the broiler. Divide the onion marmalade among the slices. Top each with a few rosemary leaves and then a slice of goat cheese. Add a sprinkling of pepper. **3** Cook the cheese toasts under the hot broiler for 3–4 minutes or until the cheese is bubbling. **4** Meanwhile, to make the dressing, whisk the oil, vinegar, and salt and pepper to taste in a mixing bowl. Add the lamb's lettuce, beets, and red bell pepper, and toss. Divide among four plates. Top with the goat cheese toasts, garnish with rosemary, and serve.

NUTRIENTS PER SERVING CAL 372 • CARBOHYDRATE 30g (sugars 12.5g) • PROTEIN 15g • FAT 22g (saturated fat 10g) • FIBER 3g • SODIUM 513mg

STILTON, PEAR, AND WATERCRESS SALAD

The ingredients of this fresh and colorful salad, with contrasting colors, textures, and flavors, are perfectly complemented by the subtle walnut oil dressing and lightly toasted walnut pieces. Serve for a tempting lunch, accompanied by crusty whole-grain rolls or bread.

WALNUT AND POPPY SEED DRESSING
½ teaspoon Dijon mustard
2 teaspoons red wine vinegar
Black pepper
1 tablespoon sunflower oil
1 tablespoon walnut oil
2 teaspoons poppy seeds

½ cup (55g) walnut pieces
1 red onion, thinly sliced
3 large, ripe pears, preferably
** red-skinned**
4 ounces (115g) watercress
4 ounces (115g) Stilton cheese, crumbled
Black pepper

PREPARATION TIME 15 minutes
SERVES 4

1 First make the dressing. Stir the mustard and vinegar together in a salad bowl with pepper to taste, then gradually whisk in the sunflower and walnuts oils. Stir in the poppy seeds. Set aside while preparing the salad. **2** Lightly toast the walnut pieces in a small frying pan, stirring them frequently. Leave to cool. **3** Add the red onion to the salad bowl and mix with the dressing. Quarter, core, and slice the pears, leaving the skins on. Add to the bowl and toss gently to coat with the dressing. **4** Add the watercress and most of the cheese and walnuts to the pears. Toss together gently, then scatter the remaining cheese and nuts over the top and serve immediately.

NUTRIENTS PER SERVING CAL 348 • CARBOHYDRATE 22g (sugars 21g) • PROTEIN 10g • FAT 26g (saturated fat 7g) • FIBER 6g • SODIUM 500mg

SUGAR SNAP SALAD WITH BLACK GRAPES AND FETA CHEESE

Sugar snap peas, with their full flavor and crisp texture, work well with baby spinach leaves and a little peppery arugula to provide the salad base for tangy feta cheese and sweet black grapes. Serve this quickly prepared lunch dish with thick slices of warm country-style or pita bread.

Grated zest and juice of 1 lemon
½ teaspoon superfine sugar
½ teaspoon Dijon mustard
Salt and black pepper
1 tablespoon extra virgin olive oil
10 ounces (300g) sugar snap peas
8 ounces (200g) seedless black grapes, halved

8 ounces (200g) feta cheese, cut into thin slices
2 ounces (45g) arugula, shredded
6 ounces (170g) baby spinach leaves

PREPARATION TIME 20 minutes
SERVES 4

1 Combine the lemon zest and juice in a large salad bowl. Add the sugar and mustard with salt and pepper to taste. Whisk the ingredients together until the sugar and salt have dissolved in the lemon juice. Whisk in the olive oil. **2** Cut the sugar snap peas across in half. Bring a large pan of water to a boil, add the sugar snap peas, and bring back to a boil. Immediately drain the sugar snaps and refresh under cold running water. Add them to the salad bowl and turn and fold to coat them with the dressing. **3** Add the grapes, feta cheese, arugula, and spinach to the bowl, and mix the salad gently but well so that all the ingredients are coated with dressing. Serve at once.

NUTRIENTS PER SERVING CAL 221 • CARBOHYDRATE 14g (sugars 13g) • PROTEIN 12g • FAT 14g (saturated fat 7g) • FIBER 3g • SODIUM 785mg

Red and black grapes are a light, appetizing treat and are thought to help protect against heart disease.

MELTED BRIE WITH VEGETABLES

In this unusual salad, a creamy dressing made from melted brie cheese and delicately flavored with tarragon is spooned over spicy roasted potato wedges, baby plum tomatoes, green beans, and red onion. It seems very indulgent, but makes a healthy main dish.

4 ounces (100g) thin green beans, halved
2 pounds (900g) baking potatoes, scrubbed
  and cut into big wedges
1½ tablespoons extra virgin olive oil
1 teaspoon paprika
1 teaspoon coarse salt
A few coarsely crushed black peppercorns
2 tablespoons sesame seeds
1 small iceberg lettuce, torn into bite-sized
  pieces
1 red onion, thinly sliced
½ cucumber, chopped

8 ounces (225g) baby plum or cherry
  tomatoes, halved
Juice of 1 lemon
Salt and black pepper

BRIE DRESSING
8 ounces (250g) brie, rind removed and diced
4 tablespoons 2 percent milk
1 tablespoon finely chopped fresh tarragon
Black pepper

PREPARATION AND COOKING TIME 1 hour
SERVES 4

1 Preheat the oven to 400°F (200°C) and put in a roasting pan to heat. Drop the beans into a large saucepan of boiling water and blanch for 2 minutes. Using a slotted spoon, scoop the beans out of the pan into a colander and refresh under cold running water. Add the potatoes to the saucepan of boiling water and cook for 3 minutes, then drain. **2** Put the potato wedges in a bowl. Add the oil, paprika, coarse salt, and crushed peppercorns; toss to coat the potatoes. Pour them into the hot roasting pan. Roast for about 15 minutes. Sprinkle with the sesame seeds and roast for another 30 minutes, turning once or twice, until crisp and browned. **3** When the potatoes are ready, remove from the oven and keep hot. Put the beans, lettuce, onion, cucumber, and tomatoes in a mixing bowl. Add the lemon juice and salt and pepper to taste, and toss well. **4** To make the dressing, combine the brie and milk in a saucepan and heat gently, stirring, until melted and well blended. Stir in the tarragon and a little pepper and cook for a few seconds. **5** Spoon the bean and tomato salad into four bowls. Top with the roasted potatoes and spoon the warm brie dressing over them. Serve at once.

NUTRIENTS PER SERVING CAL 491 • CARBOHYDRATE 48g (sugars 8g) • PROTEIN 21g • FAT 26g (saturated fat 9g) • FIBER 6g • SODIUM 673mg

the side

ON THE SIDE

Not only are **beets** rich in potassium and a good source of folate, but boiled or roasted they retain all their valuable minerals and a wealth of vitamins, including vitamin C.

BEETS IN BÉCHAMEL

Colorful, tender slices of beets are topped with crumbly chestnuts and tangy scallions, all under a satisfying white sauce.

4 beets, about 12 ounces total (85g each)
1½ teaspoons sunflower oil
6 scallions, trimmed and cut into
  2-inch (4cm) lengths
1 small clove garlic, crushed
4 ounces (115g) canned chestnuts
1 tablespoon butter

2 tablespoons all-purpose flour
¾ cup (175ml) 2 percent milk
Salt and black pepper

PREPARATION TIME 40 minutes
COOKING TIME about 1 hour
SERVES 4

1 Put the beets in a large saucepan, cover with water, and bring to a boil. Cover and simmer for about 45 minutes, until tender. Drain and set aside to cool. **2** Heat the oil in a small frying pan and sauté the scallions and garlic for 2–3 minutes until softened. Remove from the heat and stir in the chestnuts, pressing them with the back of a spoon or spatula so that they crumble slightly. **3** Trim the tops and bottoms of the beets and peel. Slice thinly and arrange in the bottom of a shallow ovenproof dish. Sprinkle with the scallion and chestnut mixture. **4** Melt the butter in a small saucepan, stir in the flour, and then gradually add the milk to make a fairly thin sauce. Add salt and pepper to taste. **5** Pour the sauce over the beets and chestnuts. **6** Preheat the broiler and set the dish under the broiler for about 5 minutes, until the top is golden and bubbly. Serve immediately.

NUTRIENTS PER SERVING CAL 150 • CARBOHYDRATE 22g (sugars 10g) • PROTEIN 4g • FAT 6g (saturated fat 3g) • FIBER 3g • SODIUM 103mg

EGGPLANT WITH TAHINI DRESSING

Lightly steamed eggplant spiked with scallions and sun-dried tomatoes are served in a Middle Eastern dressing of sesame-based tahini, making an unusual alternative to cream or butter sauces.

1 pound (400g) eggplants
4 scallions
1 ounce (25g) sun-dried tomatoes in oil (about 3 tablespoons)

FOR THE DRESSING
1 clove garlic
1 lemon

1 tablespoon tahini paste
3 tablespoons olive oil
Salt and black pepper

TO GARNISH a few sprigs of dill

TOTAL TIME 25 minutes
SERVES 4

1 Fill a steamer with water and bring it to a boil. **2** Trim the eggplants. Halve them lengthwise if they are large, then cut them widthwise into slices about ¼ inch (5mm) thick. Put them into the steamer, cover, and cook for 6–8 minutes, until they have softened. **3** To make the dressing, peel the garlic and crush it into a small bowl, then squeeze 3 tablespoons of juice from the lemon and add it to the garlic. Add the tahini paste and olive oil, season to taste, and mix. **4** Trim and thinly slice the scallions. Drain and chop the sun-dried tomatoes and set them aside. **5** Transfer the cooked eggplants to a colander and press down firmly with a spoon to remove as much of their juice as possible—do not worry if they break up. Transfer them to a serving bowl and stir in the scallions and the sun-dried tomatoes. **6** Pour over the tahini dressing and toss well. Chop enough dill to make 1 tablespoon and scatter it over the eggplants. Leave them to cool for 5 minutes to let the flavor develop before serving.

NUTRIENTS PER SERVING CAL 140 • CARBOHYDRATE 4g (sugars 2g) • PROTEIN 2g • FAT 13g (saturated fat 3g) • FIBER 2g • SODIUM 4mg

SOY-DRESSED GREEN BEANS

Young, thin beans are tossed in soy sauce with fresh ginger in this stylish side dish. If you like, substitute sliced carrots, runner beans, or baby corn, adjusting the cooking time.

1 pound (500g) green beans, trimmed
Salt
2 cloves garlic, finely chopped
½ teaspoon finely chopped ginger
2 tablespoons soy sauce
½ teaspoon sugar

PREPARATION TIME 10 minutes
COOKING TIME 5 minutes
SERVES 4

1 Line up the green beans in bunches and cut them in half crosswise. **2** Bring a saucepan of water to a boil, then add the beans and a pinch of salt and return to a boil. Reduce the heat and simmer for 3 minutes, or until the beans are tender. **3** Place the garlic, ginger, soy sauce, and sugar in a serving bowl and stir them together until the sugar has dissolved. Drain the beans, toss them into the dressing, then serve.

NUTRIENTS PER SERVING CAL 32 • CARBOHYDRATE 5g (sugars 3g) • PROTEIN 2g • FAT 1g (saturated fat 0g) • FIBER 3g • SODIUM 534mg

Cabbage may help to prevent cancer of the colon and offer relief for painful gastric ulcers. It also provides vitamins C, E, and K.

STIR-FRIED CABBAGE AND SPRING GREENS

Green cabbage contrasts with dark spring greens in this easy stir-fry, while crunchy cashew nuts, ginger, and celery add Asian flavor.

12 ounces (350g) green cabbage
12 ounces (350g) spring greens, such as spinach, beet greens, or Swiss chard
2 cloves garlic
1-inch (2cm) piece fresh root ginger
2 ribs celery
4 scallions

2 tablespoons Asian sesame oil
6 tablespoons unsalted cashew nuts

TO SERVE light soy sauce

TOTAL TIME 20 minutes
SERVES 4–6

1 Shred the cabbage and spring greens. Peel and chop the garlic, peel and grate the ginger, and slice the celery and scallions. **2** Heat the sesame oil in a large frying pan and fry the cashew nuts for 30 seconds, until they are just beginning to turn brown. **3** Add the garlic, ginger, celery, and scallions and cook them for 30 seconds, being careful not to let the garlic burn. **4** Add the cabbage and spring greens; stir-fry for 3–5 minutes, until softened but not wilted. **5** Serve sprinkled with soy sauce.

NUTRIENTS PER SERVING CAL 182 • CARBOHYDRATE 10g (sugars 7g) • PROTEIN 7g • FAT 13g (saturated fat 2g) • FIBER 6g • SODIUM 34mg

BRUSSELS SPROUT STIR-FRY

Brussels sprouts are packed with healthy vitamins, bioflavonoids, and compounds believed to ward off cancer. In this quick and delicious traditional dish, they are combined with chestnuts, which unlike other nuts are very low in fat.

1 cup (175g) canned chestnuts
1 tablespoon sunflower oil
1 leek, trimmed and finely sliced
1 pound (550g) Brussels sprouts, trimmed and finely sliced
1 cup (225ml) hot vegetable stock

Salt and black pepper

PREPARATION TIME 10 minutes
COOKING TIME 8 minutes
SERVES 4

1 Heat the oil in a wok or frying pan. Add the leek and stir-fry for 30 seconds, then add the sprouts and stir-fry over a medium heat for another 2 minutes, until the sprouts are beginning to turn brown at the edges. **2** Add the stock, reduce the heat, cover, and simmer for about 4 minutes until the sprouts are just tender but not soggy. **4** Crumble the chestnuts between your fingers and stir them into the sprouts and leeks. Cook, covered, for another minute to heat through. Add salt and pepper to taste, then serve.

NUTRIENTS PER SERVING CAL 160 • **CARBOHYDRATE 22g (sugars 8g)** • **PROTEIN 7g** • **FAT 6g (saturated fat 1g)** • **FIBER 8g** • **SODIUM 126mg**

CELERY AND APPLE

Celery is at its best in the crisp, cold days of winter when there is also a good selection of apples available. They are delicious combined with wine, herbs, and capers.

1 bunch celery
3 red apples
2–3 tablespoons olive oil
12 fresh sage leaves
1 large clove garlic
1 bay leaf

6–8 tablespoons dry white wine
2 tablespoons capers, optional
Salt and black pepper

TOTAL TIME 30 minutes
SERVES 4

1 Trim off the root end of the celery, then slice the ribs into thin semicircles, cutting across the entire bunch. Rinse and set aside. **2** Core the apples but do not peel them. Roughly chop them into cubes and set aside. **3** Generously cover the bottom of a large frying pan with olive oil, and heat it until it shows a haze. Snip the sage leaves into the pan. Peel the garlic and crush it in. Allow the sage and garlic to sizzle for a few seconds, then quickly add the celery, apples, and bay leaf and stir. **4** After 1 minute, pour in enough white wine to cover the mixture. Continue cooking over high heat, stirring occasionally, until the celery is cooked but still crunchy. If the mixture dries out before the celery is cooked, add a little more wine. **5** When the celery is cooked, stir in the capers, if using, and heat them through. Season with salt and pepper to taste, remove the bay leaf from the pan, and serve.

NUTRIENTS PER SERVING CAL 141 • CARBOHYDRATE 13g (sugars 12g) • PROTEIN 1g • FAT 7g (saturated fat 1g) • FIBER 2g • SODIUM 255mg

ORANGE AND SESAME CARROTS

The natural crunch and sweet taste of young carrots is enhanced by cooking them in orange juice. Sesame seeds provide vitamin E and calcium and a special nutty flavor.

1 pound (500g) baby carrots
1 medium orange
1 tablespoon butter or sunflower oil
Salt and black pepper

1 tablespoon sesame seeds

TOTAL TIME 25 minutes
SERVES 4

1 Peel the carrots, unless they are organic—if so, they will only need scrubbing. If they are very small, leave them whole; otherwise, cut them in half lengthwise. **2** Wash any wax off the orange, then remove the zest with a zester and squeeze out the juice. Put the orange zest and juice into a large saucepan, then add the butter and bring to a boil over medium heat. **3** Add the carrots to the saucepan, then season them to taste with salt and pepper. Bring back to a boil, then reduce the heat to medium, cover, and simmer for 10–12 minutes, shaking the pan occasionally, until the carrots are tender but not soft. **4** Meanwhile, put the sesame seeds into a frying pan and dry-fry them over a fairly high heat for about 2 minutes, shaking the pan until they are golden. **5** Stir the sesame seeds into the carrots and serve.

NUTRIENTS PER SERVING CAL 108 • CARBOHYDRATE 13g (sugars 12g) • PROTEIN 2g • FAT 6g (saturated fat 2g) • FIBER 4g • SODIUM 57mg

In addition to vitamin C, **oranges** contain pectin, which may lower blood cholesterol levels.

ITALIAN BAKED ENDIVE

Plump heads of Belgian endive and the intense Mediterranean flavors of sun-dried tomatoes, lemon, and black olives taste delicious baked beneath a crunchy crust of cheese and bread crumbs.

1 medium-thick slice of day-old bread or
⅓ cup (15g) fresh white bread crumbs
2 ounces (40g) Italian-style premium cheese,
such as Parmigiano-Reggiano cheese
6 sun-dried tomatoes in oil
4 large heads Belgian endive, each about
5 ounces (150–175g)
½ lemon
3 tablespoons olive oil
Black pepper
16 pitted black olives

TOTAL TIME 30 minutes
SERVES 4

1 Preheat the oven to 400°F (200°C). Remove and discard the crusts from the slice of bread, if using, and turn it into bread crumbs in a food processor. Grate the cheese into the bread crumbs, mix them together, and set aside. **2** Drain the sun-dried tomatoes on paper towels, then chop them and set them aside. **3** Remove any blemished outer leaves from the endive heads, neaten the bases, and cut each head into quarters lengthwise. **4** Squeeze the lemon and measure out 1 tablespoon of the juice into a large, shallow, ovenproof dish. Then stir in 2 tablespoons of the olive oil. **5** Arrange the quartered endive, cut sides up, in the ovenproof dish. Drizzle the remaining 1 tablespoon olive oil over them, then season them with black pepper. **6** Scatter the sun-dried tomatoes over the endive, followed by the black olives, then sprinkle the cheese and bread crumb mixture over the top. Bake for 15 minutes, until the topping is golden brown.

NUTRIENTS PER SERVING CAL 189 • CARBOHYDRATE 7g (sugars 1g) • PROTEIN 5g
• FAT 16g (saturated fat 4g) • FIBER 2g • SODIUM 212mg

LEMON ZUCCHINI

This is a simple but refreshing dish of thinly sliced, tender zucchini with a generous sprinkling of finely grated lemon zest, seasoned with sea salt and black pepper.

1 pound (500g) small zucchini
1½ tablespoons olive oil
1 lemon
Coarse sea salt and black pepper

TOTAL TIME 15 minutes
SERVES 4

1 Thinly slice the zucchini on the diagonal. **2** Heat the olive oil in a large frying pan, add the zucchini, and fry, stirring frequently until they are tender. **3** Meanwhile, wash any wax off the lemon and finely grate the zest. When the zucchini are cooked, sprinkle the lemon zest over them and season well with sea salt and black pepper.

NUTRIENTS PER SERVING CAL 56 • CARBOHYDRATE 2g (sugars 2g) • PROTEIN 2g • FAT 4g (saturated fat 1g) • FIBER 1g • SODIUM 1mg

Zucchini contains vitamins A and C and folate. Most of the nutrients lie in the tender, edible skin.

MINTED LETTUCE, PEAS, AND SCALLIONS

We often think of lettuce as a salad vegetable, but as this summer side dish proves, it can be delicious cooked.

2 tablespoons butter
1½ cups (225g) shelled peas, about 1½ pounds (675g) pod weight, or frozen peas
6–8 large leaves of romaine lettuce, cut into large pieces
4 scallions, trimmed and finely sliced
4–6 tablespoons vegetable stock
2 tablespoons white wine, optional

1 teaspoon sugar
1 sprig of mint
Salt and black pepper
¼ cup low-fat cream cheese, softened

PREPARATION TIME 10 minutes
COOKING TIME 15 minutes
SERVES 4

1 Melt the butter in a heavy saucepan over low heat. Add the peas, lettuce, and scallions and cook, stirring, for about 1 minute. **2** Add the stock wine (if using), sugar, mint sprig, and salt and pepper to taste. **3** Bring to a simmer, cover, and simmer for 10 minutes, until the peas are tender. **4** Remove the mint and stir in the cream cheese. Serve immediately.

NUTRIENTS PER SERVING CAL 113 • CARBOHYDRATE 4g (sugars 4g) • PROTEIN 6g • FAT 6g (saturated fat 4g) • FIBER 3g • SODIUM 54mg

An average serving of cooked **peas** provides a quarter of the vitamin C and half the thiamin your body needs every day.

DAHL

Indian cooking uses a wide variety of lentils and split peas, which are infused with flavor by simmering with spices and served as dahl—a creamy accompaniment to a vegetable curry.

12 ounces (350g) split red lentils
1 teaspoon ground turmeric
½ teaspoon chili powder
½-inch (1cm) piece fresh ginger
2 cloves garlic
½ teaspoon garam masala
Salt
2 tablespoons butter
Pinch of ground cumin
1 small onion, diced

TOTAL TIME 25 minutes
SERVES 4

1 Put a kettle of water on to boil. Pick over the lentils and remove any small pieces of grit, then put them into a sieve and rinse them under cold running water. **2** Put the lentils into a saucepan and cover with 6 cups (1.2l) boiling water from the kettle. Add the turmeric and chili powder, cover, and bring to a boil. **3** Meanwhile, peel the ginger, cut it into four thin slices, and add them to the lentils. Peel the garlic and crush it into the saucepan. As soon as the lentils reach the boiling point, reduce the heat and simmer for 10 minutes, or until the lentils are soft and almost all the liquid has been absorbed. **4** Stir in the garam masala, then add salt to taste, and cook the dahl for another 5 minutes, leaving the pan uncovered if the mixture is still soupy. **5** Meanwhile, heat the butter and cumin in a small frying pan. Add the onion and fry it gently in the spiced butter until soft. **6** Put the dahl into a heated serving dish, stir in the fried onion, and serve hot.

NUTRIENTS PER SERVING CAL 333 • CARBOHYDRATE 51g (sugars 3g) • PROTEIN 21g • FAT 6g (saturated fat 4g) • FIBER 4.5g • SODIUM 70mg

MIXED MUSHROOMS WITH BRANDY

A harmonious mixture of dried and fresh mushrooms, cooked in olive oil and their own juices with onion, garlic, fresh parsley, and a splash of brandy, makes an indulgent side dish.

Small bunch of parsley
1 ounce (25g) dried morels or cèpes
2 tablespoons butter
1 tablespoon olive oil
1 medium onion, chopped
8 ounces (200g) button chestnut mushrooms
8 ounces (200g) cremini mushrooms
4 ounces (150g) oyster mushrooms
2 cloves garlic, minced
1–2 tablespoons brandy
Salt and black pepper

TOTAL TIME 30 minutes
SERVES 4

1 Put a half-filled kettle on to boil. Chop enough parsley to make 3 tablespoons. Put the dried mushrooms into a small bowl, cover with 1 cup (200ml) boiling water, and leave to soak.
2 Meanwhile, heat the butter and olive oil in a large frying pan over medium heat. Add the onion and fry while preparing the fresh mushrooms. **3** Clean the mushrooms. Halve the button mushrooms, slice the cremini mushrooms thickly, and cut the oyster mushrooms into strips lengthwise, removing the stems if they are tough. **4** Increase the heat under the pan, then add the garlic and the mushrooms. Sauté for 5 minutes, until the mushrooms are just softened. **5** Line a sieve with paper towels and place it over a bowl. Pour the soaked mushrooms into it so that the paper catches any grit and the soaking water drains into the bowl. Reserve this liquid. Rinse and chop the drained mushrooms. **6** With a slotted spoon, lift the fried onions and mushrooms from the frying pan and put them into a bowl, leaving their juices in the pan. **7** Add the drained mushrooms and their soaking water to the pan. Boil rapidly until the liquid has a syrupy consistency. **8** Stir in the brandy. Return the onions and mushrooms to the pan, season to taste, stir in the parsley, and reheat. Transfer to a warm dish to serve.

NUTRIENTS PER SERVING CAL 126 • CARBOHYDRATE 4g (sugars 3g) • PROTEIN 5g • FAT 9g (saturated fat 4g) • FIBER 2g • SODIUM 46mg

HONEY-ROAST PARSNIPS, SQUASH, AND POTATOES

Roasting retains the nutrients and color of a variety of winter vegetables, enhanced by the addition of a sweet honey glaze sharpened with grainy mustard.

2 parsnips, peeled
1 small winter squash, such as acorn, dumpling, or buttercup squash
2 large potatoes, cut into wedges
1 tablespoon sunflower oil
2 tablespoons honey

2 teaspoons whole-grain mustard
1 tablespoon lemon juice

PREPARATION TIME 20 minutes
COOKING TIME 50 minutes
SERVES 4

1 Preheat the oven to 400°F (200°C). Halve or quarter the parsnips and remove the woody core, then cut into chunks. **2** Halve the squash and remove the seeds. Cut into wedges and peel. **3** Cook the parsnips, squash, and potatoes in boiling salted water for 2 minutes, until slightly tender. Drain well. **4** Put the oil in a shallow ovenproof dish and heat in the oven for 2–3 minutes. Add the drained vegetables, turning them to coat them in oil. Bake for about 30 minutes, until they start to look golden, turning them halfway through the cooking time. **5** Meanwhile, mix the honey with the mustard and lemon juice. When the vegetables are beginning to brown, remove them from the oven and pour the honey and mustard mixture over them. Stir to coat. **6** Return the vegetables to the oven and continue cooking for 10–15 minutes until they are deeply golden. Serve hot.

NUTRIENTS PER SERVING CAL 220 • CARBOHYDRATE 44g (sugars 22g) • PROTEIN 5g • FAT 4g (saturated fat 0.5g) • FIBER 6g • SODIUM 21mg

Pumpkins and the many varieties of winter squash, such as **acorn** and **butternut**, are particularly valuable in a vegetarian diet as rich sources of vitamin A.

POTATO AND GREEN BEAN CURRY

Tender, sliced new potatoes and thin green beans are cooked in an aromatic mixture of butter and delicate spices. Serve with rice or naan bread, or as a side dish to another curry.

1 pound (500g) small new potatoes
8 ounces (250g) thin green beans
1 tablespoon butter
3 tablespoons sunflower oil
2 small green chiles
½ teaspoon cumin seeds
½ teaspoon ground turmeric

¼ teaspoon garam masala
1 clove garlic
Salt

TOTAL TIME 30 minutes
SERVES 4

1 Scrub the potatoes and cut them into thick slices. Top and tail the green beans, then cut them into 1-inch (2.5cm) lengths. **2** Heat the butter and oil in a wide, shallow saucepan or frying pan over high heat. When they begin to sizzle, stir in the whole green chiles and the cumin seeds, turmeric, and garam masala. Peel the garlic and crush it into the pan; stir and fry for 30 seconds. **3** Add the potatoes to the pan and season with salt. Stir them until they are coated with the spiced butter and oil. **4** Stir in the beans, cover the pan, reduce the heat to medium, and cook for 15 minutes, stirring occasionally. The curry is ready as soon as the potatoes are tender.

NUTRIENTS PER SERVING CAL 197 • CARBOHYDRATE 20g (sugars 3g) • PROTEIN 3g
• FAT 12g (saturated fat 3g) • FIBER 2.5g • SODIUM 36mg

POTATOES BOULANGÈRE

Slow-baked potato dishes are tender and flavorful. This version is made with stock instead of the usual cream and cheese, making it healthier but without losing any of the flavor.

1 pound (750g) baking potatoes, peeled
2 medium onions, thinly sliced
Salt and black pepper
Freshly grated nutmeg
1–2 cloves garlic, crushed
2⅔ cups (600ml) vegetable stock

1 tablespoon low-fat margarine

PREPARATION TIME 15 minutes, plus 15
   minutes soaking and 5 minutes standing
COOKING TIME 1 hour 30 minutes
SERVES 4-6

1 Slice the potatoes by putting them through the thin blade of a food processor or use a sharp knife. Put them in a bowl with the onions, cover with cold water, and leave to soak for 15 minutes to remove some of the starch and soften the onions. **2** Preheat the oven to 350°F (180°C). Drain the potatoes and onions and pat them dry with paper towels. Arrange a layer of onions and potatoes in a shallow ovenproof serving dish. Season with salt, pepper, and nutmeg to taste, then repeat to make four or five layers in total, ending with the seasonings. **3** Stir the garlic into the stock, then pour it over the vegetables. Dot the top with the margarine. Bake for 1½ hours, or until the top is browned and the potatoes feel soft when they are pierced with a skewer. Leave the dish to stand for 5 minutes before serving.

NUTRIENTS PER SERVING CAL 161 • **CARBOHYDRATE 31g** (sugars 5g) • **PROTEIN 4g**
• **FAT 4g** (saturated fat 1g) • **FIBER 4g** • **SODIUM 98mg**

Potatoes are a healthy high-carbohydrate food that also contains protein and fiber.

The best potatoes for:

French fries—Baking

Mashing—Baking

Roasting—Baking

Salads—Waxy or all-purpose.

HOT CAJUN POTATO WEDGES

Easy-to-make spicy wedges make a tasty side dish or a flavor-packed snack. Serve with low-fat Greek-style yogurt as a dip.

2 pounds (1kg) large potatoes
1½ teaspoons sunflower oil
2 tablespoons fresh whole-wheat bread crumbs
Pinch of cayenne pepper
½ teaspoon ground cumin
1 teaspoon garlic salt
1 teaspoon paprika

1 teaspoon ground black pepper
1 teaspoon dried thyme

PREPARATION TIME 5 minutes
COOKING TIME 35–40 minutes
SERVES 4–6

1 Preheat the oven to 425°F (220°C). Scrub the potatoes, leaving the skins on, and cut each one lengthwise into eight wedges. Place them in a large mixing bowl, add the oil, and toss to coat the wedges thinly and evenly. **2** Mix together the bread crumbs, cayenne pepper, cumin, garlic salt, paprika, pepper, and thyme in a large bowl. Add the potatoes and toss until they are evenly coated. **3** Arrange the wedges in a single layer on a large nonstick baking sheet and bake for 35–40 minutes, until they are golden brown and crisp. Serve hot.

NUTRIENTS PER SERVING CAL 227 • CARBOHYDRATE 49g (sugars 1.5g) • PROTEIN 6g • FAT 2g (saturated fat 0g) • FIBER 4g • SODIUM 58mg

SWEET ROASTED SQUASH WITH SHALLOTS

Roasted vegetables are sweetened and slightly caramelized with a touch of maple syrup or honey.

2 pounds (900g) butternut squash
8 shallots
A few sprigs of thyme
1 teaspoon olive oil
2 teaspoons pure maple syrup or honey

Salt and black pepper

PREPARATION TIME 15 minutes
COOKING TIME 30–35 minutes
SERVES 4

1 Preheat the oven to 375°F (190°C). Cut the squash in half lengthwise, remove the seeds, peel, and cut the flesh into 1½-inch (3cm) cubes. Put them into a large mixing bowl. **2** Peel the shallots and add them to the squash with most of the sprigs of thyme, reserving a few to use as a garnish. **3** Mix together the oil and maple syrup and add salt and pepper to taste, then pour it into the vegetables, tossing to coat them evenly. **4** Pour the vegetables into a roasting pan and roast for 30–35 minutes, turning them occasionally, until they are tender and golden brown. Garnish with the reserved sprigs of thyme and serve.

NUTRIENTS PER SERVING CAL 112 • CARBOHYDRATE 24g (sugars 14g) • PROTEIN 3g • FAT 13g (saturated fat 3g) • FIBER 4g • SODIUM 11mg

The flavor of **honey** depends on which flowers the bees have visited—mild clover honey is particularly suitable for cooking.

LEMON-BRAISED SPINACH WITH MUSHROOMS AND CROUTONS

This swift and delicious way to serve spinach is enlivened with soy sauce and crunchy croutons.

1 pound (400g) spinach
½ lemon
8 ounces (200g) oyster mushrooms,
  thinly sliced
2 teaspoons soy sauce
3 scallions, thinly sliced
Black pepper

FOR THE CROUTONS
2 thin slices whole-wheat bread, crusts removed
½ teaspoon garlic puree or crushed garlic
Tabasco sauce

PREPARATION TIME 10 minutes
COOKING TIME 5–10 minutes
SERVES 4

1 Preheat the broiler. Rinse the spinach, remove any tough stems, and drain well. **2** To make the croutons, cut the bread into small dice. Mix the garlic puree and Tabasco sauce together in a bowl, then stir in the bread. Transfer the spiced bread to a baking sheet or broiler in a single layer and broil for 1–2 minutes, turning the croutons over occasionally, until they are golden brown. Set aside. **3** Remove a few strips of lemon zest and reserve, then squeeze out the juice. Put the lemon juice, mushrooms, soy sauce, and scallions in a saucepan over medium-high heat and cook, shaking the pan occasionally, for 2–3 minutes, until the vegetables have softened. **4** Turn the heat to high, add the spinach, and stir for 2 minutes, or until the spinach has wilted and most of the juices have evaporated. Season with pepper. Serve the spinach hot, with the croutons and reserved lemon zest scattered over the top.

NUTRIENTS PER SERVING CAL 55 • **CARBOHYDRATE 7g (sugars 2g)** • **PROTEIN 4g**
• **FAT 1g (saturated fat 0g)** • **FIBER 3g** • **SODIUM 430mg**

BABY VEGETABLES WITH SOUR CREAM

A rich, warm trio of crisp steamed vegetables makes an excellent accompaniment to a main dish, but it can also hold its own as a vegetable salad, served with hot, crusty bread.

6 ounces (175g) baby carrots
8 ounces (250g) baby zucchini
8 ounces (250g) thin asparagus spears
1 cup (200ml) sour cream
2 teaspoons whole-grain mustard

1 tablespoon salted butter at room temperature
Black pepper

TOTAL TIME 20 minutes
SERVES 4

1 Prepare a steamer by half filling the bottom pan with water and putting it on to boil.
2 Meanwhile, peel and trim the carrots and cut any large ones in half lengthwise. Trim and rinse the baby zucchini and halve them lengthwise, then trim and rinse the asparagus spears.
3 Put the carrots into the steamer, cover, and steam for 5 minutes. Then lay the zucchini over the carrots, and the asparagus over the zucchini. Replace the cover and steam for another 5 minutes.
4 While the vegetables are in the steamer, put the sour cream into a saucepan, then stir in the mustard and heat the mixture very gently until just warmed through. **5** Warm a serving bowl, put the vegetables into it, and stir in the butter and some black pepper. Pour in the warm cream dressing, stir gently to mix it in thoroughly, and serve at once.

NUTRIENTS PER SERVING CAL 170 • CARBOHYDRATE 7g (sugars 6g) • PROTEIN 5g
• FAT 14g (saturated fat 8g) • FIBER 3g • SODIUM 55mg

veg

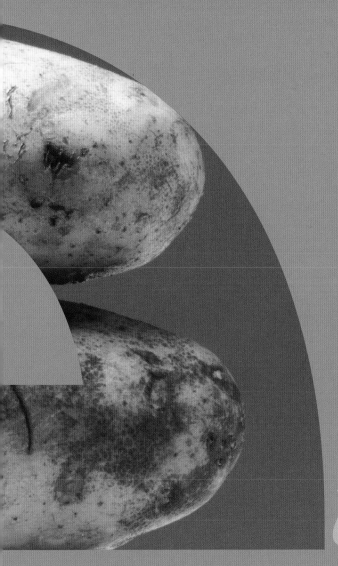

tables

as a main course

VEGETABLES

AS A MAIN COURSE

CELERY ROOT DUMPLINGS IN TOMATO BROTH

Fluffy white dumplings in a light tomato and vegetable broth make a delicious lunch or supper. Both the soup and dumplings can be made in advance, ready to be simmered just before serving.

1 red bell pepper
1 tablespoon extra virgin olive oil
1 leek, thinly sliced
1 garlic clove, crushed
4 cups (900ml) vegetable stock, preferably homemade
1 tablespoon tomato puree
1 cup (140g) frozen peas
2 tomatoes, about 4 ounces (100g) in total, skinned and roughly chopped
Salt and black pepper

TO GARNISH sprigs of basil

CELERY ROOT DUMPLINGS
1 medium celery root, peeled and diced
1⅔ cups (75g) fine fresh white bread crumbs
4 ounces (125g) soft, mild goat cheese
2 teaspoons chopped fresh basil
1 egg, beaten

PREPARATION TIME about 1 hour, plus about 15 minutes cooling
COOKING TIME about 20 minutes
SERVES 4

1 Preheat the broiler. Broil the red pepper for about 10 minutes, turning it often, until the skin is charred all over. Put it in a plastic bag and set it aside until cool enough to handle. Peel the pepper, discard the seeds, and cut the flesh into ½-inch (1cm) squares. **2** For the dumplings, cook the diced celery root in boiling water for 10–15 minutes or until very tender. Drain well, then puree in a blender or food processor, or mash until smooth. Set aside to cool. **3** Meanwhile, heat the oil in a large saucepan. Add the leek and garlic, and cook for 1 minute. Stir in the red pepper, stock, and tomato puree. Bring to a boil, then reduce the heat and simmer for 8 minutes. Add the peas halfway through the cooking. Remove from the heat. Stir in the tomatoes and seasoning to taste, then set aside. **4** Add the bread crumbs, goat cheese, basil, and egg to the celery root, with seasoning to taste. Mix well until all the ingredients are thoroughly combined. Use 2 small spoons (teaspoons are suitable) to shape the mixture into twelve small dumplings, setting them on a plate as they are made. **5** Bring a large saucepan of water to a boil. Gently lower half the dumplings, one by one, into the water on a slotted spoon. Bring the water back to a boil, then cover, reduce the heat, and simmer gently for 4–5 minutes. Use the slotted spoon to remove the dumplings from the pan to a double layer of paper towels to drain. Repeat with the remaining dumplings. **6** Return the tomato broth to the heat and bring to a boil. Ladle the soup into bowls, add the dumplings, and garnish with basil. Serve immediately.

NUTRIENTS PER SERVING CAL 225 • CARBOHYDRATE 22g (sugars 7g) • PROTEIN 12g • FAT 10g (saturated fat 4g) • FIBER 3g • SODIUM 512mg

TOMATOES WITH A SPINACH STUFFING

A generous filling of fresh spinach enriched with pine nuts and tangy cheese gives an Italian flavor to the giant tomatoes in this dish, and it is equally delicious served hot or cold.

1½ tablespoons olive oil
8 ounces (250g) fresh spinach
4 large tomatoes, about 8 ounces (225g) each
1 cup (125g) pine nuts
1 clove garlic
4 ounces (125g) Italian-style premium cheese,
    such as Parmigiano-Reggiano
Salt and black pepper

TOTAL TIME 30 minutes
SERVES 2

1 Preheat the oven to 425°F (220°C). Lightly oil a baking sheet. Remove the stems from the spinach. **2** Heat the rest of the oil in a saucepan, add the spinach, cover, and cook for 2 minutes. Uncover, stir, and leave to cook for 1 minute. Drain off the liquid, transfer the spinach to a bowl, and set it aside. **3** Rinse and dry the tomatoes; slice off and reserve the tops. Discard the pith, seeds, and juice from the center of each. **4** Lightly toast the pine nuts, then add them to the spinach. Peel the garlic and crush it in, then grate over the cheese, season to taste with salt and black pepper, and mix. **5** Press the spinach mixture into the tomatoes, piling it up, then replace the tops, balancing them on the stuffing. Bake on the top shelf of the oven for 12–15 minutes. Serve hot.

NUTRIENTS PER SERVING CAL 790 • CARBOHYDRATE 9g (sugars 8g) • PROTEIN 36g • FAT 68g (saturated fat 16g) • FIBER 5g • SODIUM 658mg

Dishes in which lime juice has
been used as a flavoring
need little salt—which can be helpful
if you are trying to follow
a low-sodium diet.

MARINATED TOFU AND MANGO KEBABS WITH GREEN MANGO SALSA

Protein-rich tofu comes alive with a Thai salsa flavored with chiles, coconut milk, and lime.

1 pound (500g) fresh tofu
1 large ripe mango, peeled and cubed

FOR THE MARINADE
1–2 fresh red chiles, seeded and chopped
2 cloves garlic, crushed
1 tablespoon grated ginger
1 tablespoon honey
Grated zest and juice of 1 lime
3 tablespoons dry sherry
2 tablespoons dark soy sauce

FOR THE SALSA
3 tablespoons coconut milk
Juice of ½ lime
**1 large green unripe mango, peeled and
   coarsely grated**
Salt

TO GARNISH lemon wedges and sliced scallions

**PREPARATION TIME 15 minutes, plus 30 minutes
   draining and 30 minutes marinating**
COOKING TIME 6–8 minutes
SERVES 4

1 Cover a large plate with several layers of paper towels. Arrange the tofu on top and cover with more paper towels, then put a plate on top and weigh it down with a can. Allow the tofu to drain for 30 minutes, then pour off the liquid and cut the tofu into 1-inch (2.5cm) cubes. **2** To make the marinade, combine all the ingredients in a shallow bowl. Add the tofu to the bowl and marinate for at least 30 minutes, stirring and turning a few times. **3** Meanwhile, make the salsa. Mix all the ingredients together with salt to taste in a small bowl and set aside. Preheat the broiler or light the grill. **4** Lift the tofu out of the marinade and thread it onto skewers alternately with the mango pieces. Add the remaining marinade to the salsa. **5** Grill the kebabs for 6–8 minutes, turning them once or twice, until the tofu is browned and heated through. Serve hot with the salsa, garnished with the strips of scallions and lime wedges.

NUTRIENTS PER SERVING CAL 230 • CARBOHYDRATE 17g (sugars 14g) • PROTEIN 16g • FAT 10g (saturated fat 6g) • FIBER 2g • SODIUM 537mg

BABY VEGETABLE FRICASSÉE

Tender poached vegetables are served in an herby béchamel sauce and given a crunchy cheese topping. They are delicious served with tagliatelle or boiled new potatoes.

1¾-pound (750g) mixture of young and baby
  vegetables such as broccoli, carrots,
  cauliflower, fennel, leeks, mushrooms,
  onions, pattypan squash or zucchini, and
  red or yellow bell peppers
2 tablespoons dry vermouth
1 bay leaf
2–3 fresh parsley stems
1 sprig thyme
Salt and black pepper
1 ounce (25g) Parmesan cheese, grated
2 tablespoons whole-wheat bread crumbs

FOR THE BÉCHAMEL SAUCE:
3 tablespoons low-fat margarine
3 tablespoons all-purpose flour
⅔ cup (150ml) 2 percent milk
3 tablespoons low-fat crème fraîche
2 tablespoons coarsely chopped fresh parsley
  or marjoram

PREPARATION TIME 15 minutes
COOKING TIME 30–35 minutes
SERVES 4

1 Prepare your chosen vegetables: trim broccoli or cauliflower into small florets; top and tail carrots; top, tail, and chop fennel finely; slice leeks thickly; slice mushrooms; cut onions into quarters; halve patty pan squash or top and tail baby zucchini; and cut peppers into squares. **2** Put 2⅔ cups (600ml) water into a large saucepan and add the vermouth, bay leaf, parsley stems, thyme, and salt and pepper. Bring to a boil. Add the vegetables, reduce the heat, and simmer for 5 minutes. **3** Using a slotted spoon, transfer the vegetables to a shallow 1½-quart (1.5l) flameproof dish. Set aside and keep warm. **4** Discard the herbs and return the vegetable stock to a fast boil. Cook, uncovered, for 10 minutes, or until it is reduced by half. Preheat the broiler. **5** To make the sauce, melt the margarine in a large saucepan and whisk in the flour. Cook for 1–2 seconds, then gradually strain in the stock. Add the milk and whisk. Bring to a boil, reduce the heat, and simmer for 3 minutes. Remove from the heat, stir in the crème fraîche and chopped herbs, and season to taste. **6** Pour the sauce over the vegetables, sprinkle the cheese and bread crumbs over the top, and place under the broiler for 2–3 minutes, until the topping is lightly browned. Serve hot.

NUTRIENTS PER SERVING CAL 279 • **CARBOHYDRATE 28g (sugars 9g)** • **PROTEIN 9g**
• **FAT 15g (saturated fat 5g)** • **FIBER 4g** • **SODIUM 146mg**

ASPARAGUS PIPERADE

In this well-traveled Spanish dish, fresh asparagus, sweet peppers, chunks of chopped tomatoes, and just enough chile to tantalize the palate are temptingly combined with fluffy scrambled eggs.

1 large onion
1 green chile
1 large red bell pepper
1 large green bell pepper
3 tablespoons olive oil
3 cloves garlic
Salt and black pepper
1 pound (500g) asparagus
1 15-ounce (400g) can diced tomatoes, drained
8 slices of bread or 4 English muffins
Butter for spreading
4 large eggs

TIME 30 minutes
SERVES 4

1 Peel the onion and slice it; seed and dice the chile; slice the bell peppers. **2** Heat the olive oil in a large frying pan or a wok with a lid. Peel the garlic, crush it into the oil, and add the onion, chile, and peppers, with salt and pepper to taste. Stir-fry them for 1 minute, then cover and cook over high heat for 3–4 minutes, shaking the pan occasionally. **3** Trim the woody ends from the asparagus, then cut each of the spears into four pieces. Add the asparagus to the onions, then cover the pan and leave them to cook for 7–8 minutes, stirring them occasionally. Preheat the broiler to high. **4** Stir the canned tomatoes into the vegetables, increase the heat, and bring the mixture to a simmer. Cook, uncovered, for 2 minutes. **5** Meanwhile, toast the bread or split and toast the English muffins and butter them. **6** Break the eggs into a bowl and beat them lightly, then add them to the vegetables and scramble them over a moderate heat, stirring, until the eggs are just set. **7** Serve surrounded by buttered toast or English muffins.

NUTRIENTS PER SERVING CAL 470 • CARBOHYDRATE 47g (sugars 13g) • PROTEIN 20g • FAT 23g (saturated fat 7g) • FIBER 5g • SODIUM 544mg

Tofu is high in protein, very low in saturated fats, and cholesterol free—an ideal ingredient in a balanced vegetarian diet.

CHINESE-STYLE TOFU OMELETS

A sweet sauce blends delicate rice wine with hoisin, garlic, and green peas in this traditional Chinese omelet. If you can't find silken tofu, use plain tofu, which is slightly firmer and drier.

1⅓ pounds (600g) silken tofu, firm or soft
3 large eggs
3–4 scallions, chopped
Salt and black pepper
2 tablespoons vegetable oil

FOR THE SAUCE
¾ cup (175ml) vegetable stock

2 tablespoons hoisin sauce
2 tablespoons Chinese rice wine or dry sherry
1 clove garlic, crushed
1 cup (150g) peas, defrosted if frozen

PREPARATION TIME 10 minutes
COOKING TIME 30–35 minutes
SERVES 4

1 Preheat the oven to 250°F (121°C) to keep the omelets warm. **2** Mash the tofu with a fork in a large bowl until it is thoroughly broken down, then beat in the eggs and scallions and season generously with salt and pepper. **3** Heat ½ tablespoon of the oil in a large nonstick frying pan until it is very hot. Add a quarter of the tofu mixture to the pan to make two omelets at a time, keeping them well apart. Fry them for 3–4 minutes on each side, until they have turned golden brown, turning them carefully because the mixture breaks up easily. **4** Transfer the omelets to a heatproof plate as they are made and put them in the oven to keep warm. Repeat the process three more times, adding oil to the pan as necessary, to make eight omelets in total. **5** After all the omelets have been made, add the vegetable stock to the pan and scrape up any caramelized cooking juices on the bottom, then bring the liquid to a boil. Stir in the hoisin sauce, Chinese rice wine, garlic, and peas and let them simmer for 2–3 minutes, until the sauce has thickened slightly and the flavors have combined. Adjust the seasoning to taste. **6** Lay two omelets on each plate, pour the sauce over them, and serve while they are still hot.

NUTRIENTS PER SERVING CAL 304 • **CARBOHYDRATE 9g (sugars 2g)** • **PROTEIN 26g** • **FAT 18g (saturated fat 5g)** • **FIBER 2g** • **SODIUM 400mg**

TOFU STIR-FRY WITH CASHEWS

Soft tofu soaks up the flavor of a tangy Asian-style marinade of soy sauce and dry sherry. It is then stir-fried with a crisp mixture of vegetables and cashew nuts and served with noodles.

FOR THE MARINADE
2 cloves garlic
1½ tablespoons tamari
2 tablespoons dry sherry
1½ teaspoons Asian sesame oil
1 teaspoon brown sugar
Black pepper

FOR THE STIR-FRY
10 ounces (280g) tofu
½-inch (1cm) piece fresh root ginger
1 cup (150g) sugar snap peas
4 ounces (100g) fresh shiitake mushrooms
1 large red or yellow bell pepper
12 ounces (400g) Chinese cabbage or
**   romaine lettuce**
1 bunch of scallions
3 tablespoons peanut oil
12 ounces (250g) thin Chinese egg noodles
Salt
⅔ cup (85g) roasted cashews

TOTAL TIME 30 minutes
SERVES 4

1 Preheat the oven to 250°F (121°C) and boil a kettle of water. To make the marinade, peel the garlic and crush it into a bowl. Add the tamari, sherry, sesame oil, brown sugar, and pepper and stir. **2** Drain the tofu and cut it into rectangles ½ inch (1cm) thick. Add it to the marinade and leave it to soak. **3** Peel and finely chop the ginger. Top and tail the sugar snap peas. Clean the mushrooms and slice them thinly. Quarter the pepper, stack the pieces, and slice them into long strips. Set them all aside. **4** Remove any damaged outer leaves from the cabbage and cut it across into ½-inch (1cm) slices. Trim and slice the scallions. **5** Heat 1 tablespoon of the oil in a frying pan over medium heat. Drain the tofu, reserving the marinade, stir-fry it for 3 minutes, then remove and keep warm. **6** Heat the remaining 2 tablespoons oil in the pan. Add the ginger, sugar snap peas, and mushrooms and stir-fry for 2 minutes. Then add the sliced pepper, stir-fry for 2 minutes more, add the cabbage and the scallions, and stir-fry for another 2 minutes. **7** Put the noodles into a bowl, add salt, and cover with boiling water. Stir gently, cover, and set aside for as long as instructed on the package. **8** While the noodles are soaking, pour the reserved marinade into the vegetables, add the cashews, and stir for 1–2 minutes, until the marinade is hot. **9** Stir the tofu into the vegetables and keep warm. Drain the noodles. Serve mixed with the vegetables.

NUTRIENTS PER SERVING CAL 574 • CARBOHYDRATE 58g (sugars 10g) • PROTEIN 24g • FAT 30g (saturated fat 7g) • FIBER 7g • SODIUM 400mg

SPICED CARROT AND CHICKPEA FRITTERS

These vivid, healthy carrot and chickpea patties are whipped together in a food processor with fresh herbs and strong spices to produce a fresh-tasting variation on the veggie burger.

12 ounces (350g) carrots
1 clove garlic
1 large bunch of fresh cilantro
1 15-ounce (400g) can chickpeas
1½ teaspoons ground cumin
1½ teaspoons ground coriander
1 large egg
2 tablespoons all-purpose flour
Oil for frying

TO SERVE hamburger buns and salad

TOTAL TIME 20 minutes
SERVES 4

1 Coarsely grate the carrots and set them aside. **2** Peel and roughly chop the garlic. Chop enough cilantro to make 6 tablespoons. **3** Drain and rinse the chickpeas and put them into a food processor with the garlic, cilantro, cumin, and coriander. Process to a rough paste. Add the carrot, egg, and flour and process briefly until evenly mixed but slightly chunky. **4** Heat the oil in a frying pan and divide the mixture into eight fritters. Fry in batches for 2–3 minutes on each side, until golden. Drain on paper towels. Serve in buns with salad. If necessary, you can make the fritters in advance and fry them later.

NUTRIENTS PER SERVING CAL 223 • CARBOHYDRATE 25g (sugars 7g) • PROTEIN 9g • FAT 10g (saturated fat 2g) • FIBER 6g • SODIUM 223mg

SPINACH AND CELERY ROOT ROULADE

Celery root has a mild celery-like flavor and an appealing crunchy texture. Combined with spinach, crème fraîche, and a touch of Cheddar, it makes an elegant roulade.

12 ounces (350g) fresh spinach, washed and tough stems removed
1 tablespoon butter
3 tablespoons low-fat crème fraîche
4 large eggs, separated
1 ounce (25g) aged Cheddar cheese, grated
Salt and black pepper

FOR THE FILLING
1 small celery root, peeled and finely grated
1 tablespoon lemon juice
4 tablespoons low-fat cream cheese, softened
2 tablespoons reduced-fat mayonnaise

PREPARATION TIME 30 minutes
COOKING TIME 15 minutes
SERVES 4

1 Heat the oven to 375°F (190°C). Line a 15-inch by 11-inch (33cm by 23cm) jelly-roll pan with parchment paper. Put the spinach into a large saucepan, cover tightly, and cook over a moderate heat for a few minutes, shaking the pan occasionally, until wilted. Drain well, then chop finely. **2** Heat the butter in a small saucepan and add the chopped spinach. Cook gently until any excess liquid has evaporated. Remove from the heat and leave to cool. **3** Add the crème fraîche, egg yolks, and cheese to the spinach, with salt and pepper to taste. In a clean bowl, whisk the egg whites until stiff, then fold them into the spinach-and-egg mixture. Spoon into the prepared pan and smooth the surface using a palette knife. **4** Bake for 10–15 minutes, until firm to the touch and golden. Turn out onto a sheet of waxed paper and peel away the lining paper. While still warm, carefully roll up the roulade in the waxed paper and place it seam side down on a cooling rack. **5** Meanwhile, to make the filling, put the celery root into a bowl and sprinkle with lemon juice. Add the cream cheese, mayonnaise, and some salt and pepper and mix well. **6** Unroll the roulade, remove the waxed paper, and spread with the celery root mixture. Roll up again and transfer the roulade carefully to a serving dish. Serve warm or chill. If not serving the roulade immediately, let it come to room temperature about 30 minutes before serving.

NUTRIENTS PER SERVING CAL 250 • CARBOHYDRATE 5g (sugars 4g) • PROTEIN 14g • FAT 16g (saturated fat 6g) • FIBER 4g • SODIUM 407mg

If you don't enjoy the soggy texture of cooked spinach, try it as a salad vegetable instead. It's rich in vitamin C, potassium, folate, and vitamin K.

BLACK BEAN CHILI

The rich, smoky flavor of this dish goes well with an herbed rice—try lemon, garlic, and dill in it.

1 pound (500g) black beans
1 bay leaf
2 tablespoons cumin seeds
2 tablespoons dried oregano
½ teaspoon cayenne pepper
1–2 tablespoons chili powder
1 tablespoon paprika
2 tablespoons sunflower oil
2 cups (350g) chopped onion
6 cloves garlic, chopped
1 15-ounce (400g) can diced tomatoes

½ teaspoon Liquid Smoke, optional
Salt
2 tablespoons red wine vinegar

TO GARNISH chopped fresh cilantro

PREPARATION TIME 15 minutes, plus overnight soaking
COOKING TIME 1½–2½ hours
SERVES 8 as part of a buffet

1 Soak the beans overnight in water to cover. Next day, drain them, cover with fresh water, bring to a boil, and cook for 15 minutes. Drain again, add 5 cups (1.2l) fresh water and the bay leaf, and bring to a boil, then simmer for 20 minutes. **2** Meanwhile, heat a small, heavy frying pan. Add the cumin seeds; when they begin to darken, add the oregano and stir for 10 seconds. Take the pan off the heat, stir in the cayenne pepper, chili powder, and paprika, then crush to a powder with a pestle and mortar. **3** Heat the oil in a frying pan over medium heat and cook the onions for 5 minutes. Add the garlic and fry for 1 minute, then add the spices and cook for another 2 minutes, stirring. **4** Add the tomatoes with their juice and the Liquid Smoke, if using, and cook the sauce over medium heat for 2 minutes. **5** Pour the spiced tomato sauce into the beans and simmer for 30 minutes to 1 hour 30 minutes, depending on the age of the beans (older beans take longer to cook), until they are thoroughly soft but not breaking apart. Add more boiling water during cooking if necessary and stir occasionally to ensure they do not burn on the bottom. Add salt and extra cayenne to taste. **6** Just before serving, stir in the vinegar and garnish with chopped cilantro. *Tip:* Liquid Smoke, available in some supermarkets, adds an unusual, smoky overtone to food, but use it sparingly.

NUTRIENTS PER SERVING CAL 490 • CARBOHYDRATE 77g (sugars 11g) • PROTEIN 31g • FAT 8g (saturated fat 1.5g) • FIBER 12g • SODIUM 62mg

Fresh chiles have more vitamin C than citrus fruits, but their often violent spiciness limits the amount the body can tolerate.

BEAN AND MUSHROOM BURGERS

These hearty, lightly spiced vegetarian burgers are made with red kidney beans and red onions and served with pita bread, salad, and a sweet red onion relish.

1 15-ounce (400g) can red kidney beans
2 medium red onions, about 8 ounces (200g)
in total
4 tablespoons olive oil
2 tablespoons red wine vinegar
2 tablespoons raw sugar, such as muscovado
8 ounces (200g) button mushrooms
1 clove garlic
1 tablespoon garam masala
2 tablespoons whole-wheat flour
1 small bunch of fresh mint
Salt and black pepper

TO SERVE 4 pita breads and green salad

TOTAL TIME 30 minutes
SERVES 4

1 Rinse the beans well and spread them out on a dish towel to drain. Peel the onions. **2** To make the red onion relish, heat 1 tablespoon of olive oil in a saucepan. Slice one of the onions thinly and add it to the pan with the vinegar and sugar. Bring to a boil, stirring, then reduce the heat and leave it to simmer, uncovered, for 15–20 minutes, until the onion is softened and slightly sticky, stirring it from time to time. Then remove the pan from the heat and keep it warm. **3** Meanwhile, quarter the other onion, and put it into a food processor. Clean the mushrooms, add them to the onion, and process until finely chopped. Alternatively, chop them both finely by hand. **4** Heat another tablespoon of olive oil in a frying pan, add the onion-and-mushroom mixture, and cook over a medium-high heat, stirring occasionally for 5–8 minutes, until golden and dry. **5** Peel the garlic, crush it into the mushroom mixture, stir in the garam masala and flour, and cook for 1 minute. Chop enough mint to make 2 tablespoons. Remove the pan from the heat, add the mint, and season well with salt and pepper. **6** Put the kidney beans on a deep plate and mash them firmly with a potato masher, then stir in the cooled mushroom mixture. **7** Divide the mixture into four and, with lightly floured hands, shape each serving into a burger. **8** Heat the remaining 2 tablespoons of oil in a large frying pan, add the bean burgers, and cook them over medium-high heat for 6–8 minutes, turning them once, until they are well browned. Warm the pita breads. **9** Arrange the burgers on a warm dish or individual plates and spoon the onion relish over the tops. Serve with the warm pitas and a green salad.

NUTRIENTS PER SERVING CAL 461 • CARBOHYDRATE 73g (sugars 15g) • PROTEIN 15g
• FAT 13g (saturated fat 2g) • FIBER 9g • SODIUM 665mg

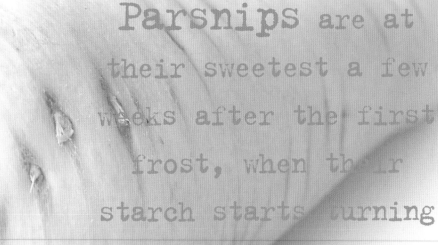

Parsnips are at their sweetest a few weeks after the first frost, when their starch starts turning to sugar.

VEGETABLE STEW WITH DUMPLINGS

Casseroles and stews are popular winter staples, when hearty root vegetables provide warming, sustaining nourishment; they're even better with dumplings.

1 tablespoon olive oil
1 tablespoon butter
8 ounces (225g) baby or pickling onions, peeled
2 carrots, cut into wedges
1 small parsnip, peeled and cut into chunks
1 small rutabaga, peeled and cut into chunks
12 ounces (350g) potatoes, peeled and halved
  or quartered
2 cups (225g) cooked or canned chestnuts
1¾ cups (400ml) vegetable stock
1 sprig of thyme

Salt and black pepper
6 ounces (175g) green beans

FOR THE DUMPLINGS
1⅓ cups (175g) self-rising flour
2 tablespoons chopped fresh parsley
Pinch of salt
6 tablespoons butter

PREPARATION TIME 30 minutes
COOKING TIME 1¼ hours
SERVES 4

1 Heat the oil and butter in a large flameproof casserole or Dutch oven and fry the onions for 2–3 minutes, until just beginning to brown. **2** Add the carrots, parsnip, and rutabaga and sauté gently over a low heat for 2–3 minutes. Cover and cook over a low heat for 6–8 minutes. **3** Add the potatoes, chestnuts, stock, and thyme. Add salt and pepper, then cover and cook over very low heat for 30–40 minutes. Meanwhile, prepare the green beans. If using runner beans, top and tail and string, if necessary. Slice thinly using a sharp knife or bean slicer. For green beans, top and tail. Add the beans to the stew and cook for another 5 minutes. **4** To make the dumplings, put the flour and parsley into a bowl. Add the salt and rub in the butter. Stir in enough water to make a soft dough, then shape the dough into eight small dumplings. **5** Arrange the dumplings on top of the vegetables. Cover tightly and cook gently for another 10–15 minutes, until the dumplings are well risen and fluffy. Serve at once.

NUTRIENTS PER SERVING CAL 600 • CARBOHYDRATE 86g (sugars 18g) • PROTEIN 11g
• FAT 26g (saturated fat 14g) • FIBER 10g • SODIUM 400mg

EGGPLANT ROLLS

Unlike many eggplant recipes, which swim in oil, this one has just enough extra virgin olive oil to enrich and enhance the vegetables. A great cook-ahead dish, this is delicious with crusty bread or baked potatoes and salad.

1 large eggplant, about 12 ounces (340g), cut lengthwise into 10 slices, each about ⅛ inch (3mm) thick
2 tablespoons extra virgin olive oil
1 onion, thinly sliced
4 garlic cloves, chopped
½ red bell pepper, seeded and cut into thin strips
½ green bell pepper, seeded and cut into thin strips
1 zucchini, cut into thin strips
2 tablespoons chopped fresh parsley
6 tomatoes, diced

Pinch of sugar
6 tablespoons tomato puree
4 tablespoons chopped fresh basil
6 ounces (170g) mozzarella cheese, diced
8 black olives, pitted and chopped
Salt and black pepper

TO GARNISH sprigs of basil

PREPARATION TIME 45 minutes
COOKING TIME 30 minutes
SERVES 4

1 Dice the two outer (end) slices of eggplant, with the peel, and set aside to add to the filling. Use 2 teaspoons of the olive oil to brush the remaining eight eggplant slices sparingly on both sides. Heat a ridged griddle or heavy frying pan and brown the eggplant slices for about 2 minutes on each side or until they are tender but not soft. Set aside on a board. **2** Add the remaining oil to the pan and cook the onion, half of the garlic, the red and green peppers, zucchini, and reserved diced eggplant for about 5 minutes, or until softened. Add the parsley and half of the diced tomatoes, and continue to cook for another 5–6 minutes. **3** Season the vegetable mixture, add the sugar, and pour in the tomato puree. Bring to a boil, then cover and cook over low heat for about 10 minutes, or until the mixture is richly flavored and thickened. **4** In a bowl, combine the remaining garlic and diced tomatoes with the chopped basil, mozzarella, and olives. Set this topping mixture aside. Preheat the oven to 350°F (180°C). **5** Lightly season the eggplant slices. Place a generous serving of the vegetable filling at the wider end of one slice and roll up to enclose the filling. Repeat with the remaining eggplant slices and filling, placing the rolls side by side in an ovenproof dish. **6** Spoon the tomato and mozzarella mixture evenly over the top. Bake for about 30 minutes or until the cheese topping has melted. Garnish with basil sprigs and serve hot or warm.

NUTRIENTS PER SERVING CAL 245 • CARBOHYDRATE 11g (sugars 10g) • PROTEIN 14g • FAT 16g (saturated fat 7g) • FIBER 5g • SODIUM 237mg

BAKED EGGPLANT AND APPLE LAYERS

Serve this versatile dish, with its fresh tomato sauce, as a main course or as an accompaniment.

1 pound (500g) eggplant, cut into ½-inch
  (1cm) slices
Salt and black pepper
12 ounces (300g) tart firm apples, cored and
  cut into ¼-inch (5mm) slices

FOR THE SAUCE
2 cloves garlic, crushed
2 tablespoons olive oil
2 tablespoons chopped fresh flat-leaved parsley
1 tablespoon chopped fresh thyme

2 tablespoons tomato puree
1 pound (500g) plum tomatoes, peeled,
  seeded, and chopped

TO GARNISH 1 tablespoon chopped fresh herbs,
  such as parsley and thyme

PREPARATION TIME 15 minutes, plus
  30 minutes standing
COOKING TIME 40 minutes
SERVES 4

1 Sprinkle both sides of the eggplant slices with salt, place them in a colander, and set aside to drain for 30 minutes. **2** To make the sauce, put all the ingredients in a food processor or use a handheld mixer, and blend until smooth. Set aside. **3** Preheat the oven to 425°F (220°C) and heat a ridged cast-iron griddle or heavy frying pan over medium-high heat. Rinse the eggplant slices and dry them with paper towels. Dry-fry them for 2–3 minutes on each side, until they have softened and browned. **4** Arrange half the eggplant slices in a single layer in an 8-inch (25 by 20cm) ovenproof dish and cover them with 2 tablespoons of the sauce, spreading it out evenly. Layer all the apple slices on top and cover with another 2 tablespoons of sauce. Top with the remaining eggplants and smooth the remaining sauce over the top. Bake for 30 minutes. **5** Sprinkle the dish with the herbs and serve, hot or at room temperature.

NUTRIENTS PER SERVING CAL 132 • CARBOHYDRATE 17g (sugars 14g) • PROTEIN 3g
• FAT 7g (saturated fat 1g) • FIBER 5g • SODIUM 33mg

MEXICAN VEGETABLE AND CORNMEAL PIE

Break through the crisp golden brown cornmeal topping of this spicy pie to discover a delicious mixture of tastes and textures. Feel free to substitute your own favorite ingredients.

1 tablespoon sunflower oil
1 rib celery, chopped
1 large clove garlic, crushed
1 cup (150g) chopped onion
½ green bell pepper, chopped
1 teaspoon cayenne pepper
1 15-ounce (400g) can red kidney beans, drained and rinsed
12 green olives, pitted and sliced
1 tablespoon chopped jalapeño peppers
⅔ cup (75g) fresh or frozen corn
1 15-ounce (400g) can chopped tomatoes
1 tablespoon tomato puree
Salt and black pepper

FOR THE TOPPING
1 cup (25g) cornmeal or polenta
1 tablespoon all-purpose flour
2 teaspoons baking powder
½ teaspoon salt
1 egg, beaten
1 cup (100ml) skim milk, plus more as needed
2 tablespoons grated low-fat Cheddar cheese

PREPARATION TIME 20 minutes, plus 5 minutes standing
COOKING TIME 1 hour
SERVES 4

1 Preheat the oven to 400°F (200°C). Heat the oil in a saucepan over high heat. Stir in the celery, garlic, onion, and green pepper, bring them to a sizzle, then cover, reduce the heat to low, and cook for 10 minutes, or until they have softened. Stir in the cayenne pepper and cook for another 1–2 minutes. **2** Stir in the kidney beans, olives, jalapeño peppers, corn, canned tomatoes, and tomato puree. Add salt and pepper to taste. Bring the mixture to a boil and simmer for 5 minutes. Then spoon the mixture into a large ovenproof serving dish. **3** To make the topping, mix together the cornmeal, flour, baking powder, and salt. Beat in the egg and milk. The mixture should look like a thick batter; if not, add 1–2 tablespoons of milk. **4** Spoon the topping over the vegetables, sprinkle with the cheese, and bake for 40 minutes, or until the topping is risen and golden brown. Let the pie stand for 5 minutes before serving.

NUTRIENTS PER SERVING CAL 378 • CARBOHYDRATE 56g (sugars 12g) • PROTEIN 19g • FAT 10g (saturated fat 3g) • FIBER 8g • SODIUM 900mg

Boiling **broccoli** almost halves its vitamin C content, so it is better to microwave, stir-fry, or lightly steam it.

SPICY BROCCOLI AND CAULIFLOWER

Spicy and crisp, this delicious combination of broccoli and cauliflower with capers and pickled green peppercorns is finished off with a tasty double-cheese and bread crumb topping.

5 cloves garlic
1 green chile
2 tablespoons olive oil
1 pound (500g) broccoli florets
1 pound (500g) cauliflower florets
Salt and black pepper
2 ounces (50g) Emmental cheese

2 ounces (50g) Cheddar cheese
3 tablespoons dried bread crumbs
2 tablespoons capers
1–2 tablespoons pickled green peppercorns

TOTAL TIME 25 minutes
SERVES 4

1 Preheat the broiler and put a kettle of water on to boil. **2** Peel and thinly slice the garlic. Seed and chop the chile. **3** Heat the oil in a frying pan or large wok with a lid. Add the garlic and chile, stir in the broccoli and cauliflower florets, sprinkle with salt and pepper, and add ¾ cup (150ml) boiling water. Cover the pan and cook the vegetables over high heat for 4–5 minutes, until they are tender. Stir or toss them halfway through cooking. Drain well. **4** Meanwhile, grate the Emmental and Cheddar cheeses and mix them with the bread crumbs. **5** Stir the capers and peppercorns into the vegetables. Transfer them to a shallow flameproof dish, sprinkle the cheese and bread crumb mixture over the top, and place under the broiler until the cheese melts and the topping turns golden. Serve hot.

NUTRIENTS PER SERVING CAL 286 • CARBOHYDRATE 16g (sugars 6g) • PROTEIN 20g • FAT 16g (saturated fat 6g) • FIBER 6g • SODIUM 507mg

CHUNKY VEGETABLE CRUMBLE

A tasty mixture of root vegetables and creamy butter beans topped with a savory cheese crumble makes a nourishing dish. Sunflower seeds in the crumble add texture and extra protein.

1 tablespoon sunflower oil
1 onion, sliced
2 garlic cloves, crushed
3 carrots, cut into ¾-inch (2cm) chunks
2 parsnips, cut into ¾-inch (2cm) chunks
8 ounces (250g) baby turnips, quartered
12 ounces (350g) waxy new potatoes,
  scrubbed and cut into ¾-inch (2cm) chunks
2 cups (450ml) vegetable stock
Generous dash of Worcestershire sauce
1 tablespoon tomato paste
2 bay leaves
1 14-ounce (410g) can butter beans or lima
  beans, drained and rinsed

3 tablespoons chopped fresh parsley
Salt and black pepper

FOR THE TOPPING
⅔ cup (85g) whole-wheat flour
2 tablespoons chilled butter, diced
3 ounces (75g) aged Cheddar cheese,
  coarsely grated
1 ounce (30g) sunflower seeds

PREPARATION TIME 40 minutes
COOKING TIME 20 minutes
SERVES 4

1 Heat the oil in a large saucepan, add the onion, and cook gently for 10 minutes or until softened. Add the garlic and cook for another minute. **2** Add the carrots, parsnips, turnips, and potatoes. Stir in the stock, Worcestershire sauce, tomato paste, and bay leaves. Bring to a boil, then reduce the heat, cover, and simmer for 20 minutes, stirring occasionally. **3** Meanwhile, make the crumble topping. Put the flour in a bowl and rub in the butter. Sprinkle over 1½ tablespoons cold water and mix together with a fork to make large crumbs. Stir in the cheese and sunflower seeds. Set aside. **4** Preheat the oven to 375°F (190°C). Stir the butter beans into the vegetables and cook for another 5–7 minutes, until the vegetables are just tender. Remove and discard the bay leaves. **5** Remove a large ladleful of the vegetables and stock, and mash until smooth or puree in a blender or processor. Stir the puree into the vegetable mixture in the pan to thicken it slightly. Stir in the parsley, and season with salt and pepper to taste. **6** Spoon the vegetable mixture into a lightly greased 1½-quart (1.7l) ovenproof dish. Sprinkle the crumble mixture evenly over the top. Bake for 20 minutes or until golden brown. Serve hot.

NUTRIENTS PER SERVING CAL 465 • CARBOHYDRATE 55g (sugars 16g) • PROTEIN 17g • FAT 21g (saturated fat 9g) • FIBER 12.5g • SODIUM 673mg

ROASTED VEGETABLE TART

A scattering of fresh herbs and melted cheese add the finishing touches to vegetables baked in a crisp filo crust. You can vary it with a mixed bread crumb and grated hard cheese topping.

1 pound (400g) eggplant
1 pound (400g) zucchini
1 red bell pepper, thickly sliced
1 yellow bell pepper, thickly sliced
1 cup (150g) thickly sliced red onion
1 clove garlic, chopped
1 teaspoon chopped fresh rosemary or thyme, plus extra sprigs for topping
3 tablespoons olive oil

Salt and black pepper
4 sheets filo pastry, about 4 ounces (125g) total
2 ounces (75g) part-skim mozzarella cheese, shredded

PREPARATION TIME 15 minutes
COOKING TIME 50–70 minutes
SERVES 4

1 Preheat the oven to 400°F (200°C). Cut the eggplant and zucchini into ½-inch (1cm) slices. Arrange all the vegetables in a single layer in a roasting pan, scatter the garlic and rosemary over them, then drizzle with 2 tablespoons of the olive oil. Season to taste. 2 Roast the vegetables for 40–60 minutes until they have softened and browned. 3 Meanwhile, place a baking sheet in the oven to warm. Line an 8–9-inch (20–23cm) tart pan with a removable bottom with the sheets of filo pastry, brushing each layer with oil before adding the next. Crumple up any overhanging edges to form a rim. Place the tart pan on the baking sheet and bake the pastry shell for 5–8 minutes, until golden brown. 4 Reduce the oven to 325°F (160°C). Spoon the roasted vegetables into the pastry shell and scatter the cheese and chopped rosemary evenly over the top. Return the tart to the oven for 10 minutes, or until the cheese has just melted. Cut into quarters and serve it warm.

NUTRIENTS PER SERVING CAL 260 • CARBOHYDRATE 28g (sugars 10g) • PROTEIN 10g • FAT 12g (saturated fat 3g) • FIBER 4.5g • SODIUM 81mg

MEDITERRANEAN CHICKPEA PIE

Enjoy the taste of the Mediterranean with vegetables and chickpeas cooked in red wine, tomatoes, and Italian herbs, topped with flavored mashed potatoes. Serve with a seasonal green vegetable, such as Savoy cabbage.

2 tablespoons extra virgin olive oil
2 onions, chopped
2 celery ribs, chopped
1 red bell pepper, seeded and diced
2 garlic cloves, crushed
2 zucchini, sliced
2 15-ounce (410g) cans chickpeas, drained and rinsed
2 15-ounce (410g) cans chopped tomatoes
2 tablespoons sun-dried tomato paste
¾ cup (150ml) red wine
2 teaspoons dried Italian herb seasoning
Salt and black pepper

FOR THE POTATOES
2 pounds (1kg) potatoes, peeled and cut into chunks
4 tablespoons 2 percent milk
1 large egg
2 ounces (50g) Italian-style premium cheese, such as Parmigiano-Reggiano, freshly grated
⅓ cup (50g) sun-dried tomatoes in oil, drained and finely chopped
3 tablespoons chopped fresh basil

PREPARATION TIME 55 minutes
COOKING TIME 25 minutes
SERVES 6

1 Heat 1 tablespoon of the oil in a large pan; add the onions, celery, red bell pepper, and garlic, and sauté for 5 minutes. Add the zucchini, chickpeas, tomatoes with their juice, tomato paste, wine, and dried herbs. Season with salt and pepper to taste and mix well. **2** Bring to a boil, then reduce the heat. Cover the pan and simmer for 20 minutes, stirring occasionally. Uncover the pan, increase the heat, and cook for another 10–15 minutes, stirring occasionally, until the liquid has thickened slightly. **3** Meanwhile, cook the potatoes in a saucepan of boiling water for 15–20 minutes, until tender. Preheat the oven to 400°F (200°C). **4** Drain the potatoes well, then return to the pan. Add the milk and the remaining 1 tablespoon olive oil, and mash until smooth. Beat in the egg, cheese, sun-dried tomatoes, chopped basil, and salt and pepper to taste. Mix well. **5** Spoon the vegetable mixture into an ovenproof dish. Top with the mashed potatoes, covering the vegetables completely. Mark the top of the potatoes decoratively with a fork. **6** Bake the pie for 25 minutes, or until the potato topping is nicely browned. Serve hot.

NUTRIENTS PER SERVING CAL 426 • CARBOHYDRATE 54g (sugars 12g) • PROTEIN 18g • FAT 15g (saturated fat 3.5g) • FIBER 8g • SODIUM 404mg

Celery may lower cholesterol and high blood pressure and contains an anti-inflammatory agent that can help to alleviate the painful symptoms of gout.

pa

ta
and grains

PASTA AND GRAINS

VEGETABLE PRIMAVERA

The secret of this dish lies in the light cooking of a mixture of fine spring vegetables, which gives them a crisp texture and fresh flavor, and contrasts well with the stuffed pasta.

8 ounces (200g) baby carrots
1 cup (150g) baby corn
8 ounces (200g) young thin green beans
Salt and black pepper
8 ounces (250g) baby or small zucchini
Small handful of fresh parsley or chervil
1 pound (400g) fresh ricotta and spinach tortellini

1 tablespoon olive oil
½ lemon
1 tablespoon whole-grain mustard

TOTAL TIME 30 minutes
SERVES 4

1 Put a large saucepan of water and a kettle on to boil. Preheat the oven to 250°F (121°C). 2 Trim the carrots, corn, and beans, and cut them into short lengths if they are large. Plunge the vegetables into the pan of boiling water, add salt, bring back to a boil, then simmer for 4–5 minutes, keeping them slightly crisp. 3 Meanwhile, trim the zucchini. Cut baby zucchini in half lengthwise, small ones into slices, and set aside. Chop the parsley. 4 Lift the cooked vegetables from the boiling water with a slotted spoon, put them into a bowl, and keep them warm in the oven. Bring the water back to a boil, adding more water from the kettle if necessary. Add the pasta and boil gently for 5–6 minutes. 5 Meanwhile, heat the olive oil in a large saucepan, add the zucchini and fry them, stirring continuously, for 2–3 minutes. 6 Squeeze the lemon juice into the zucchini, then add the drained vegetables, mustard, and salt and pepper to taste. Toss gently together. 7 Drain the pasta and mix it into the vegetables. Turn into a warmed serving dish, add a sprinkling of parsley, and serve hot.

NUTRIENTS PER SERVING CAL 537 • CARBOHYDRATE 53g (sugars 11g) • PROTEIN 26g • FAT 25g (saturated fat 13g) • FIBER 7g • SODIUM 615mg

RADIATORE WITH FLAGEOLET BEANS IN TOMATO DRESSING

Beans and pasta eaten together provide an excellent source of protein. Here, tender flageolet beans partner chunky pasta shapes in a salad with celery, red pepper, and canned artichoke hearts. A well-flavored dressing marries the ingredients perfectly.

8 ounces (225g) radiatore or other pasta shape
1 15-ounce (400g) can artichoke hearts, drained and quartered
4 ripe tomatoes, skinned and cut into thin wedges
3 celery ribs, thinly sliced
1 red bell pepper, seeded and cut into thin strips
1 14-ounce (400g) can flageolet or navy beans, drained and rinsed
2 tablespoons finely shredded fresh basil

TOMATO DRESSING
2 tablespoons sun-dried tomato paste
1 garlic clove, crushed
2 tablespoons extra virgin olive oil
2 tablespoons lemon juice
1 teaspoon superfine sugar
Salt and black pepper

PREPARATION TIME 25–35 minutes, plus cooling
SERVES 4

1 Cook the pasta in boiling water for 10–12 minutes, or according to the package instructions, until al dente. Drain the pasta thoroughly and turn it into a large bowl. **2** Add the artichoke hearts, tomatoes, celery, red bell pepper, flageolet beans, and basil. Gently toss the pasta and vegetables together. The cold vegetables will cool the pasta, keeping the pieces firm and separate, while the warmth of the pasta will bring out the flavors of the vegetables. **3** Whisk all the ingredients for the dressing together until thoroughly blended. Add seasoning to taste and pour the dressing over the salad. Lightly toss the salad to coat all the ingredients with dressing, then set aside until cool. Transfer the salad to individual bowls or one large dish to serve.

NUTRIENTS PER SERVING CAL 400 • CARBOHYDRATE 68g (sugars 10g) • PROTEIN 18.5g • FAT 7.5g (saturated fat 1.5g) • FIBER 9g • SODIUM 438mg

STUFFED GIANT PASTA SHELLS

A creamy sauce of zucchini, low-fat ricotta, and walnuts reinterprets an Italian classic and makes a sophisticated dressing for pasta shells filled with a spinach-and-herb stuffing.

1 pound (500g) spinach, trimmed
3 zucchini, thinly sliced
4 garlic cloves, chopped
2 cups (500ml) vegetable stock
8 ounces (250g) ricotta cheese
¾ cup (100g) walnuts, coarsely chopped
3 ounces (85g) Italian-style premium cheese, such as Parmigiano-Reggiano, freshly grated
3 tablespoons chopped fresh chervil or marjoram
3 tablespoons chopped fresh chives or 3 small shallots, finely chopped

3 tablespoons chopped fresh basil
1 egg, lightly beaten
Salt and black pepper
12 giant pasta shells for stuffing
2 ounces (55g) Edam cheese, grated
2 tablespoons finely shredded fresh basil, or tiny basil leaves

PREPARATION TIME 40 minutes, plus 5 minutes standing
COOKING TIME 30 minutes
SERVES 4

1 Wash the spinach well and place the wet leaves in a large saucepan. Cover and cook over a high heat for about 3 minutes, shaking the pan frequently. When the spinach is just tender and wilted, transfer it to a colander and leave it to drain and cool. 2 Meanwhile, place the zucchini and half the garlic in a saucepan. Pour in the stock and bring to a boil. Cook over high heat for about 3 minutes, or until the zucchini are just tender. 3 Puree the zucchini and stock in a blender or food processor until smooth, adding half the ricotta cheese, the walnuts, 2 tablespoons of the cheese, and seasoning to taste. The resulting sauce should have a consistency halfway between light and heavy cream, slightly more runny than a coating sauce should be. 4 When the spinach is cool enough to handle, squeeze it dry in small handfuls and chop it coarsely. Mix the spinach with the chervil, chives, basil, the remaining garlic and ricotta cheese, the egg, and seasoning to taste. 5 Preheat the oven to 375°F (190°C). Use a small teaspoon to stuff the pasta shells with the spinach mixture, and arrange them in an ovenproof dish. 6 Pour the sauce over the stuffed shells and sprinkle with the remaining grated cheese. Cover the dish tightly with foil and bake for 30 minutes. 7 Sprinkle the Edam cheese and basil over the cooked stuffed pasta and leave to stand for 5 minutes, uncovered, until the cheese melts, then serve.

NUTRIENTS PER SERVING CAL 630 • CARBOHYDRATE 39g (sugars 6g) • PROTEIN 34g • FAT 38g (saturated fat 13g) • FIBER 5.5g • SODIUM 865mg • SALT 2g

BAKED RIGATONI WITH EGGPLANT

Eggplant adds flavor and texture to a hearty vegetarian pasta dish topped with a crisp layer of bread crumbs and cheese. The rich tomato sauce could be made in advance, then the dish quickly assembled and baked as required. Serve with a green salad.

2 tablespoons extra virgin olive oil
1 large onion, chopped
2 garlic cloves, crushed
4 tablespoons red wine
2 15-ounce (400g) cans chopped tomatoes in thick tomato juice
5 sun-dried tomatoes packed in oil, drained and chopped
1 eggplant, cut into ½-inch (1cm) cubes
2 tablespoons chopped fresh oregano

8 ounces (225g) rigatoni or other chunky pasta tube shape, such as penne
⅔ cup (30g) fresh whole-wheat bread crumbs
1 ounce (30g) Italian-style premium cheese, such as Parmigiano-Reggiano, freshly grated
Salt and black pepper

PREPARATION TIME 35 minutes
COOKING TIME 15–20 minutes
SERVES 4

1 Heat the oil in a large saucepan, add the onion, and cook gently for 4–5 minutes, stirring frequently, until it has softened and turned lightly golden. Add the garlic and cook gently for another 1–2 minutes. **2** Pour in the wine and allow it to bubble for a few minutes, then add the canned tomatoes with their juice, the sun-dried tomatoes, eggplant, and oregano. Bring to a boil, then reduce the heat, cover, and simmer gently for 15–20 minutes, stirring occasionally.
3 Meanwhile, cook the pasta in a large pan of boiling water for 10–12 minutes, or according to the package instructions, until al dente. Drain well. **4** Preheat the oven to 400°F (200°C). Season the tomato sauce with salt and pepper to taste. Transfer the cooked pasta into a large, lightly greased ovenproof dish. Pour over the sauce and mix together well so that all the pasta is coated.
5 Combine the bread crumbs and cheese in a bowl, and sprinkle this mixture evenly over the top of the pasta. Bake for 15–20 minutes, or until the sauce is bubbling and the top is golden brown and crisp. Serve hot.

NUTRIENTS PER SERVING CAL 425 • CARBOHYDRATE 59g (sugars 12g) • PROTEIN 14g • FAT 15g (saturated fat 3g) • FIBER 6g • SODIUM 200mg

KASHTOURI

This Egyptian dish of rice, macaroni, and lentils in a spicy tomato sauce makes a quick light meal.

¾ cup (150g) risotto rice, such as arborio
Salt and black pepper
5 ounces (150g) short-cut macaroni
2 teaspoons olive oil
1 cup (150g) chopped onion
2 large cloves garlic, crushed
1 teaspoon cayenne pepper or paprika
1 teaspoon ground coriander

1 15-ounce (400g) can diced tomatoes
2 cups (400g) cooked green lentils, including
  cooking liquid

TO GARNISH 2 tablespoons chopped fresh parsley

PREPARATION TIME 5 minutes
COOKING TIME 20 minutes
SERVES 4

1 Bring a large saucepan of water to a boil, add the rice and a pinch of salt. Return the water to a boil, then reduce the heat and simmer for 5 minutes. Add the macaroni and stir, increase the heat to medium, and cook for another 10 minutes, until both rice and macaroni are tender. Drain and set aside in a colander. 2 Meanwhile, combine the oil and 2 tablespoons water in a saucepan, add the onions and garlic, and sauté for 5 minutes, until they have softened. Stir in the spices and cook for another minute. 3 Add the tomatoes and lentils and their liquid to the onions, season to taste, and bring the mixture to a boil. Reduce the heat and simmer for 10 minutes, stirring occasionally. 4 Mix in the rice and macaroni, then add the parsley, reserving a small amount for garnish, and heat through. Serve hot, garnished with parsley.

NUTRIENTS PER SERVING CAL 450 • CARBOHYDRATE 81g (sugars 6g) • PROTEIN 17g
• FAT 7g (saturated fat 1g) • FIBER 6g • SODIUM 47mg

CATALAN-STYLE PASTA IN TOMATO BROTH

Make pasta Spanish style—in a thick fresh sauce enlivened by the flavor of herbs. Make as a side dish or as a light meal in its own right.

1 pound (500g) tomatoes, chopped
1 whole head garlic, separated into individual
 cloves and peeled
1 cup (150g) chopped onion
2-inch (5cm) strip orange zest
2 bay leaves and 2 sprigs fresh thyme, tied
 together
10–12 threads saffron
2⅔ cups (600ml) vegetable stock
1 pinch of superfine sugar
1 tablespoon olive oil
8 ounces (225g) vermicelli, broken into pieces
Salt and black pepper

TO GARNISH sprigs of fresh basil

PREPARATION TIME 20 minutes
COOKING TIME 30 minutes
SERVES 4

1 Combine the tomatoes, garlic, onions, orange zest, herbs, saffron, stock and sugar in a saucepan and bring to a boil. Cover, reduce the heat, and simmer for 20 minutes. **2** Discard the herbs and zest, then puree the broth in a food processor or with a handheld mixer. **3** Return the puree to the pan and stir in the oil, vermicelli, and salt and pepper to taste. Bring to a boil and then simmer, uncovered, for 8–10 minutes, stirring occasionally, until the pasta is cooked and the broth has thickened. Season to taste and serve, garnished with fresh basil.

NUTRIENTS PER SERVING CAL 280 • CARBOHYDRATE 55g (sugars 8g) • PROTEIN 7g
• FAT 4g (saturated fat 1g) • FIBER 3.5g • SODIUM 313mg

FETTUCCINE WITH BROCCOLI

A buttery Dijon mustard sauce with basil and parsley makes an unusual spicy dressing for ribbon noodles of fresh egg pasta, crunchy green florets of fresh broccoli, and bright cherry tomatoes.

10 fresh basil leaves
3 sprigs of parsley
2 scallions
2 small cloves garlic
2 tablespoons Dijon mustard
½ cup (125g) butter, softened
2 large crowns broccoli, about 1 pound (550g)
1 tablespoon olive oil
Salt and black pepper
1 pound (500g) fresh fettuccine or tagliatelle

TO GARNISH 10 cherry tomatoes

TIME 20 minutes
SERVES 4

1 Put a large saucepan of water on to boil for the pasta. Finely chop the basil and parsley. Trim the scallions. Finely slice the green tops and set them aside, then slice the rest. Peel and crush the garlic. **2** Blend the mustard and butter in a bowl, then stir in the herbs, white part of the scallions, and garlic, crushing them against the bottom of the bowl to release their flavors. Set aside. **3** Trim the broccoli into florets. Add the oil, salt, pasta, and broccoli to the boiling water, return to a boil, and cook for 4 minutes, or until the pasta is al dente. **4** Meanwhile, halve the cherry tomatoes. **5** Thoroughly drain the pasta and broccoli. Quickly melt the flavored butter in the pasta pan. Return the pasta and broccoli to the pan and toss them gently in the butter over medium heat until the pasta is well coated, but do not allow it to fry. **6** Transfer the pasta onto a serving platter, season, and garnish with the green scallion tops and tomatoes.

NUTRIENTS PER SERVING CAL 651 • CARBOHYDRATE 73g (sugars 5g) • PROTEIN 20g • FAT 32g (saturated fat 17g) • FIBER 4g • SODIUM 239mg

TAGLIATELLE WITH SUMMER VEGETABLES

Choose vegetables at the peak of freshness for this light pasta dish, which uses lemon, tarragon, and garlic to bring out their delicate flavors. It's perfect for a light lunch or supper on a hot day.

6 ounces (250g) thin asparagus
4 ounces (150g) green beans
4 ounces (200g) small zucchini
4 ounces (150g) young leeks
Salt and black pepper
1 pound (500g) fresh egg tagliatelle or other thin pasta
1 tablespoon olive oil

1 clove garlic, finely chopped
4 tablespoons lemon juice, or to taste
2 teaspoons chopped fresh tarragon
2–3 tablespoons finely chopped fresh flat-leaved parsley

PREPARATION TIME 15 minutes
COOKING TIME 15–20 minutes
SERVES 4

1 Put two saucepans of water on to boil. Trim off the woody stems of the asparagus and cut the spears into 1-inch (2.5cm) lengths. Trim the green beans and cut them in half. Slice the zucchini thinly. Trim and cut the leeks into quarters lengthwise, then into ½-inch (1cm) slices. **2** Put the asparagus and beans into one pan of boiling water and cook for 4 minutes, or until just tender. Drain, refresh them with cold water, and set aside. **3** Add the pasta to the remaining pan of boiling water and cook according to the instructions on the package. **4** Meanwhile, heat the olive oil in a wok or heavy nonstick frying pan over medium-high heat. Add the garlic and sauté for 30 seconds, then add the zucchini and leeks and sauté for 3 minutes, or until the zucchini are tender but not too soft. **5** Add the asparagus and beans to the wok and sauté for 1 minute, then mix in the lemon juice and tarragon. Remove from the heat and season with salt and pepper to taste. **6** Drain the pasta, reserving some of the cooking water. Stir the pasta into the vegetables, using a few teaspoons of the cooking water to moisten, if necessary. Sprinkle with the parsley and extra black pepper and serve.

NUTRIENTS PER SERVING CAL 400 • CARBOHYDRATE 73g (sugars 6g) • PROTEIN 18g • FAT 7g (saturated fat 0.5g) • FIBER 3g • SODIUM 37mg

Pasta is an excellent source of slow-release carbohydrates for sustained energy.

FLAGEOLET BEAN AND LENTIL LASAGNA

This colorful main dish is built up with layers of red pepper, lentil-and-bean sauce, sheets of lasagna, and sliced artichoke hearts. The creamy topping is a combination of cheeses.

FOR THE SAUCE
1 tablespoon sunflower oil
1 large red onion, thinly sliced
⅔ cup (100g) split red lentils
2 large red bell peppers, seeded and diced
1 large carrot, thinly sliced
2 celery ribs, thinly sliced
2½ cups (550ml) vegetable stock
1 bay leaf
2 15-ounce (410g) cans flageolet or navy
    beans, drained and rinsed
Salt and black pepper

FOR THE LASAGNA
About 12 no-precook lasagna sheets
1 15-ounce (400g) can artichoke hearts in
    water, drained, rinsed, and sliced
⅔ cup (150g) ricotta cheese
⅖ cup (100ml) 2 percent milk
3 tablespoons freshly grated Italian-style
    premium cheese, such as Parmigiano-Reggiano

**PREPARATION TIME 45 minutes, plus 5 minutes
    standing**
COOKING TIME 40 minutes
SERVES 6

1 To make the sauce, heat the oil in a saucepan over low heat. Add the onion and cook gently for 10 minutes, or until softened. Add the lentils, red bell peppers, carrot, celery, stock, and bay leaf. Bring to a boil, then reduce the heat and simmer for about 25 minutes, or until the lentils and vegetables are very tender. **2** Remove the bay leaf, then puree in a blender or food processor or by using a handheld blender directly in the pan, until smooth. Season with salt and pepper to taste, and stir in the beans. **3** Preheat the oven to 375°F (190°C). Spoon about one-quarter of the sauce over the bottom of a large, greased ovenproof dish. Cover with one-third of the lasagna sheets, then top with half of the remaining sauce. Arrange half the sliced artichoke hearts over the sauce. Repeat with another layer of pasta, then the rest of the sauce and the rest of the artichokes. Finish with the last of the pasta sheets. **4** Put the ricotta cheese into a bowl and stir in the milk until smooth. Season with pepper to taste. Spoon the ricotta sauce over the lasagna, then scatter the grated cheese on top. **5** Bake for 40 minutes, or until the sauce is bubbling and the top is golden. Remove from the oven and let stand for 5 minutes before serving.

NUTRIENTS PER SERVING CAL 400 • CARBOHYDRATE 65g (sugars 15g) • PROTEIN 21g
• FAT 8g (saturated fat 3g) • FIBER 11g • SODIUM 829mg

CHARRED VEGETABLE COUSCOUS WITH CHILLED TOMATO SAUCE

Lightly charred vegetables and herbs lend a brilliant flavor to this easy-to-make couscous dish.

FOR THE SAUCE
2 tablespoons sherry vinegar or white wine vinegar
4 teaspoons sugar
3 cups (700ml) tomato puree
1 pound (450g) plum tomatoes
2 tablespoons chopped fresh basil

FOR THE COUSCOUS
1½ cups (250g) couscous
3 red bell peppers
1 medium leek
6 ounces (200g) zucchini
1 fennel bulb
1 tablespoon olive oil
Juice of 2 lemons
8 fresh mint leaves, shredded
2 tablespoons chopped fresh parsley
Salt and black pepper

TO GARNISH ¾ cup (200g) Greek-style yogurt, fresh basil leaves

PREPARATION TIME 30 minutes
COOKING TIME 20 minutes
SERVES 6

1 Preheat the broiler. Put the couscous into a large heatproof bowl and pour 1¾ cups (400ml) of boiling water over it. Stir and let stand for 20 minutes. **2** Meanwhile, make the sauce. Heat the vinegar and sugar in a small saucepan, stirring until the sugar has dissolved, then allow this syrup to cool a little. **3** Pour the tomato puree into a large bowl. Dice the tomatoes and add them to the bowl with the basil and the vinegar syrup. Season with salt and plenty of black pepper, then chill until required. **4** Cut the peppers in half lengthwise and broil them, cut side down, until the skin is well blackened. Transfer them to a bowl, cover it with plastic wrap and leave it to cool for 2–3 minutes. **5** Thickly slice the leek and zucchini and cut the fennel into thin wedges, chopping and reserving any leaves. Spread out the leek, zucchini, and fennel wedges on the broiler pan, brush them all over with oil, and broil for 5–10 minutes, until lightly browned, turning them over halfway through cooking and removing each piece as soon as it is done. **6** When the peppers are cool enough to handle, skin and seed them, then dice the flesh and add it to the couscous, along with the other vegetables. Stir in the lemon juice, mint, parsley, and fennel leaves, and season to taste. **7** Serve the couscous at room temperature. Pile it in mounds on individual dishes, surround with a moat of chilled tomato sauce, spoon a little yogurt onto the sauce, and garnish with basil leaves.

NUTRIENTS PER SERVING CAL 234 • CARBOHYDRATE 40g (sugars 19g) • PROTEIN 7g • FAT 6g (saturated fat 2g) • FIBER 4.5g • SODIUM 152mg

VEGETABLE COUSCOUS

Sweet winter vegetables and beans, mingled with dried apricots and hot spices for a Middle Eastern flavor, make a warm and comforting stew to serve with couscous.

1 small onion
1 tablespoon butter
1 tablespoon olive oil
2 small carrots
½ small rutabaga
1 medium parsnip
1 pinch of cayenne pepper
1 pinch of turmeric
½ teaspoon ground ginger
½ teaspoon ground cinnamon
1 pinch of saffron threads, optional
Salt and black pepper
⅓ cup (50g) ready-to-eat dried apricots
⅓ cup (60g) frozen peas
⅔ cup (100g) canned chickpeas
¾ cup (125g) couscous

TO GARNISH 2 sprigs of fresh cilantro

TOTAL TIME 30 minutes
SERVES 2

1 Put a kettle of water on to boil. Chop the onion. Heat the butter and olive oil in a large Dutch oven. Add the onion and fry gently until soft. **2** Meanwhile, peel the carrots, rutabaga, and parsnip. Cut them into ½-inch (1cm) chunks and add them to the onions as you go. Stir in the cayenne pepper, turmeric, ginger, cinnamon, and the saffron threads, if using, and season to taste with salt and black pepper. **3** Chop the apricots and add them with the peas. Drain, rinse, and add the chickpeas. Add 1⅓ cups (300ml) boiling water and bring mixture back to a boil. Reduce the heat, cover, and simmer for 15 minutes. **4** Meanwhile, pour 1 cup (225ml) boiling water into a saucepan, add the couscous, and stir it, then turn off the heat and let stand, covered, until the vegetables are ready. **5** Check the couscous and season to taste. Break it up with a fork and transfer it to a serving dish. **6** Taste and adjust the seasoning of the vegetables, then spoon them and their broth over the couscous. Garnish the dish with the cilantro and serve.

NUTRIENTS PER SERVING CAL 480 • **CARBOHYDRATE 75g (sugars 28g)** • **PROTEIN 13g** • **FAT 15g (saturated fat 5g)** • **FIBER 12g** • **SODIUM 170mg**

SUMMER TABBOULEH

Bulgur is perfect with crisp, just cooked summer vegetables mixed with handfuls of fresh herbs and tossed with a lively honey-and-mustard dressing to give it an extra bite.

1½ cups (250g) bulgur (cracked wheat)
5 ounces (200g) thin green beans
1¼ cups (200g) frozen peas
Salt
5 large scallions
10 ounces (300g) tomatoes
1 lemon
1 large handful of fresh parsley leaves
1 large handful of fresh mint leaves
1 large handful of chives or dill

FOR THE DRESSING
3 tablespoons extra virgin olive oil
1 tablespoon red wine vinegar
1 teaspoon honey
1 tablespoon Dijon mustard
Salt and black pepper

TO SERVE lettuce leaves

TOTAL TIME 30 minutes
SERVES 4

1 Put a kettle of water on to boil. Combine the bulgur in a saucepan with 3 cups (700ml) cold water. Bring to a boil, reduce the heat, and simmer for 8–10 minutes, until the bulgur has absorbed all the water. **2** Meanwhile, top and tail the green beans and chop them into 1-inch (2.5cm) pieces. Put them into a saucepan with the frozen peas. Cover with boiling water, add a little salt, return to a boil, cook for 1–2 minutes, then drain. **3** Trim and thinly slice the scallions. Dice the tomatoes. Wash any wax from the lemon, grate the zest, and squeeze the juice. Add them all to the bulgur and fluff up the mixture with a fork. **4** Add the beans and peas to the tabbouleh. Chop the herbs and add them. **5** To make the honey-and-mustard dressing, whisk all the ingredients together in a bowl, then pour it over the tabbouleh and mix well, then serve with lettuce leaves.

NUTRIENTS PER SERVING CAL 382 • CARBOHYDRATE 60g (sugars 8g) • PROTEIN 12g
• FAT 11g (saturated fat 1.5g) • FIBER 4.5g • SODIUM 13mg

BULGUR PILAF WITH NUTS AND SEEDS

Although high in fat, nuts and seeds are extremely nutritious, and just a handful gives a pleasing crunch. Bulgur makes a satisfying base for this pilaf and adds fiber and B vitamins.

1 cup (150g) thinly sliced onion
3½ cups (800ml) vegetable stock
1¾ cups (300g) bulgur
3 tablespoons unsalted raw cashew nuts
3 tablespoons pumpkin seeds
1 tablespoon sesame seeds
1 pomegranate, or 1 apple, or 6 apricots

2 tablespoons chopped fresh mint
Salt and black pepper

TO GARNISH sprigs of mint

PREPARATION TIME 10 minutes
COOKING TIME 20 minutes
SERVES 4

1 Sweat the onions in 2 tablespoons of the stock over a medium-high heat for 2–3 minutes, stirring occasionally, until the onions have softened and the liquid has evaporated. Preheat the broiler. **2** Stir the bulgur and the remaining stock into the pan and bring to a boil. Cover and simmer gently over a low heat, stirring occasionally, for 12–15 minutes, until the bulgur is tender and the liquid has been absorbed. **3** Meanwhile, toast the cashew nuts under the broiler for 30 seconds, or until they are golden. Place the pumpkin and sesame seeds in a small frying pan and dry-fry them for 3–5 seconds over high heat, shaking the pan until the seeds begin to pop. Stir all the nuts and seeds into the bulgur. **4** Cut the pomegranate into quarters and scoop the seeds and juice into the bulgur. If pomegranates are not available, add chopped apple or apricots instead. Stir in the mint and adjust the seasoning to taste. Serve hot or at room temperature, garnished with sprigs of mint.

NUTRIENTS PER SERVING CAL 390 • **CARBOHYDRATE 67g (sugars 9g)** • **PROTEIN 12g** • **FAT 10g (saturated fat 1g)** • **FIBER 2.5g** • **SODIUM 294mg**

POLENTA WITH A RICH MUSHROOM SAUCE

Satisfying Italian cornmeal is topped with a dark sauce combining dried and fresh mushrooms in this luxurious main-course dish. Serve it on its own or as an accompaniment to other foods.

2½ cups (300g) instant polenta
2 teaspoons salt

FOR THE MUSHROOM SAUCE
1 ounce (20g) dried wild mushrooms
2 tablespoons olive oil
4 cloves garlic, roughly chopped
2 pounds (1kg) button or chestnut mushrooms, or a mixture of the two, thickly sliced
1 tablespoon tomato puree
2 teaspoons dried thyme

¼ cup (50ml) red wine
5 teaspoons brandy
Salt and black pepper

TO GARNISH chopped fresh parsley and sprigs of thyme

PREPARATION TIME 10 minutes, plus 30 minutes soaking
COOKING TIME 30 minutes
SERVES 4

1 Put a kettle on to boil. Put the dried mushrooms in a heatproof bowl, cover with boiling water, and let them soak for 30 minutes. **2** Meanwhile, heat the olive oil in a large saucepan over a medium-high heat. Add the garlic and sauté for 15 seconds, then add the fresh mushrooms and continue sautéing for 10 minutes, or until they have wilted. **3** Strain the soaking liquid off the wild mushrooms through a fine sieve lined with muslin or paper towels, and add 4 tablespoons of it to the cooked mushrooms. **4** Roughly chop the wild mushrooms and add them to the pan with the tomato puree, thyme, wine, and brandy. Season to taste and simmer, covered, for 20 minutes, or until you have a thin, richly flavored sauce. **5** Meanwhile, combine the polenta and salt in a large saucepan and pour in 7 cups (1.4l) water, whisking continuously to prevent any lumps. Bring the mixture to a boil, then simmer for 10 minutes, stirring frequently, until it becomes firm but not stiff. **6** Arrange spoonfuls of the polenta on individual plates, spoon the mushroom sauce alongside, and garnish with the parsley and thyme.

NUTRIENTS PER SERVING CAL 377 • CARBOHYDRATE 58g (sugars 1g) • PROTEIN 12g • FAT 8g (saturated fat 1g) • FIBER 2g • SODIUM 1006mg

SQUASH AND TALEGGIO RISOTTO

This tasty risotto makes an excellent family meal. The combination of rice and fresh vegetables, gently cooked with white wine, stock, and rosemary, with creamy Italian taleggio cheese stirred in at the end, creates a nutritious dish packed with flavor. Serve with a green leafy salad to make a complete meal.

2 tablespoons extra virgin olive oil
6 shallots, chopped
2 garlic cloves, crushed
1 large butternut squash, peeled, seeded, and diced
2 cups (450ml) vegetable stock
1¼ cups (225g) risotto rice, such as arborio
8 ounces (225g) button or chestnut mushrooms, sliced
1 cup (250ml) dry white wine
1 tablespoon chopped fresh rosemary
8 ounces (225g) taleggio cheese, rind removed and cheese diced
Salt and black pepper

TO GARNISH sprigs of rosemary

PREPARATION TIME 20 minutes
COOKING TIME 35 minutes
SERVES 4

1 Heat the oil in a large saucepan over medium-high heat, add the shallots and garlic, and cook for 2 minutes, or until the shallots begin to soften. Add the squash and cook for another 10 minutes, stirring occasionally. **2** Meanwhile, heat the vegetable stock in a saucepan to just the simmering point. Reduce the heat so the stock stays hot. **3** Add the rice to the squash and cook for 1 minute, stirring. Stir in the mushrooms, then add the wine and chopped rosemary. Bring it to a boil and bubble gently until most of the wine has been absorbed, stirring frequently. **4** Add a ladleful of the hot stock and simmer until it has been absorbed, stirring frequently. Continue adding the stock gradually, in this way, waiting for each addition to be absorbed before adding more. When all the stock has been added, the rice should be tender but still firm, and the risotto should have a creamy texture. Season with salt and pepper to taste. **5** Remove the risotto from the heat. Add the cheese and stir in gently until it starts to melt. Garnish with fresh rosemary sprigs and serve immediately.

NUTRIENTS PER SERVING CAL 513 • CARBOHYDRATE 50g (5g sugars) • PROTEIN 18g • FAT 22g (saturated fat 10g) • FIBER 2g • SODIUM 506mg • SALT 1.2g

The staple food for more than half the world's population, **rice** is an important source of starchy carbohydrate.

Best rice for:
Chinese dishes—short-grain rice
general cooking—long-grain rice
Japanese dishes—sticky brown rice
Indian dishes—basmati rice
risotto dishes—arborio rice
Thai dishes—Thai or jasmine rice
puddings—short-grain rice

TOMATO RISOTTO

A simple risotto of fresh and sun-dried tomatoes is an easy dish for a light lunch or supper.

1 tablespoon olive oil
⅓ cup (60g) finely chopped onion or shallots
1 clove garlic, crushed
2¼ cups (500ml) tomato juice
1 cup (200g) risotto rice, such as arborio
1 tablespoon tomato puree
4 ounces (100g) plum tomatoes, peeled, seeded, and diced
3 sun-dried tomatoes, drained, dried, and cut into strips

2 tablespoons fresh torn basil leaves
Salt and black pepper

TO GARNISH a few fresh basil leaves
TO SERVE 2 ounces (50g) Italian-style premium cheese, grated, such as Parmigiano-Reggiano

PREPARATION TIME 10 minutes
COOKING TIME 30 minutes
SERVES 4

1 Heat the oil in a large nonstick saucepan over low heat. Add the onion and garlic and sauté gently for 10 minutes, or until they are softened but not colored. 2 Bring the tomato juice to a simmer in a saucepan. 3 Add the rice to the onions and cook for another 1–2 minutes, stirring frequently, until the rice becomes transparent. 4 Add a small ladleful of tomato juice to the rice mixture and stir continuously until all the juice has been absorbed. Repeat, stirring after each ladleful of juice has been added, and cook for 10–15 minutes, until the rice is tender and has a creamy consistency, adding more water if necessary. 5 Stir the tomato puree, fresh and sun-dried tomatoes, and basil leaves into the rice and season to taste. 6 Serve garnished with basil and pass around the grated cheese separately.

NUTRIENTS PER SERVING CAL 288 • CARBOHYDRATE 46g (sugars 6g) • PROTEIN 10g • FAT 8g (saturated fat 3g) • FIBER 1.5g • SODIUM 396mg

EMERALD RISOTTO

Young leaves of baby spinach have a vivid color and an extra-fresh flavor that is packed with goodness. Try this risotto for a healthy supper that requires little from the cook except stirring.

5 cups (1.2l) vegetable stock, or 4
  tablespoons vegetable bouillon powder
5 tablespoons white wine
8 ounces (250g) baby spinach
4 tablespoons virgin olive oil
1 small onion
2 cloves garlic

1¾ cups (350g) risotto rice, such as arborio
Salt and black pepper
Whole nutmeg for grating

TOTAL TIME 30 minutes
SERVES 4

1 Bring the stock to a boil in a saucepan, or stir the bouillon powder into 5 cups (1.2l) boiling water. Add the wine, reduce the heat, and leave to simmer. **2** Chop the spinach leaves roughly and set them aside. **3** Heat the oil in a large saucepan or wok. Finely chop the onion and garlic and fry them gently for 2–3 minutes, until soft but not brown. Then add the rice and sauté until the grains are translucent and coated with oil. **4** Add a ladleful of stock, adjust the heat to maintain a gentle boil, and stir until most of the liquid has been absorbed. Keep adding stock, a ladleful at a time, and stir constantly for about 15 minutes, until the rice is almost cooked. **5** Add the spinach and more stock and boil and stir until the rice is cooked—risotto rice should retain a bite, but the mixture should be soft and creamy. **6** Season to taste with salt, pepper, and some freshly grated nutmeg. Serve straight from the pan.

NUTRIENTS PER SERVING CAL 448 • CARBOHYDRATE 73g (sugars 2g) • PROTEIN 8g
• FAT 14g (saturated fat 2g) • FIBER 2g • SODIUM 680mg

CURRIED LENTIL AND VEGETABLE PILAF

Curries usually take a long time to prepare and cook, but by using ready-prepared vegetables and ginger and garlic bottled in oil, this one-dish meal, rich in protein and other essential nutrients, can be on the table in half an hour.

1 cup (100g) coconut cream
3 cups (900ml) vegetable stock or water
2 tablespoons sunflower oil
1½ teaspoons cumin seeds
2 teaspoons ground coriander
1 teaspoon bottled chopped ginger in oil or syrup, drained
1 teaspoon bottled chopped garlic in oil, drained
½ teaspoon cayenne pepper, or to taste
1 cup (200g) basmati rice, rinsed
1⅛ cups (200g) red lentils

1 pound (500g) prepared mixed vegetables, such as carrots, beans, broccoli, and cauliflower
Salt and black pepper

TO GARNISH chopped fresh cilantro or parsley

TO SERVE 2 bananas, finely grated zest of 1 lime, lime juice to taste

PREPARATION AND COOKING TIME about 30 minutes
SERVES 4

1 Grate the creamed coconut into a saucepan and add the stock. Bring to a simmer over medium heat, stirring occasionally until the coconut has melted. **2** Meanwhile, heat the oil in a large Dutch oven or frying pan with a lid. Add the cumin seeds and sauté over medium-high heat until they begin to sizzle and give off their aroma. Stir in the coriander, ginger, garlic, and cayenne pepper and sauté for about 1 minute. **3** Stir in the rice, lentils, and vegetables. Pour in the coconut stock and stir to mix everything together. Bring to a boil, then reduce the heat to low, cover, and simmer for 20 minutes, without removing the lid, until the rice and lentils are tender and all the liquid has been absorbed. **4** Just before the pilaf finishes cooking, slice the bananas into a bowl. Add the lime zest and sprinkle with lime juice to taste. **5** When the pilaf is ready, adjust the seasoning if necessary and fluff up the rice with a fork. Sprinkle with the chopped cilantro and serve at once, with the bananas.

NUTRIENTS PER SERVING CAL 560 • CARBOHYDRATE 87g (sugars 18g) • PROTEIN 20g • FAT 16g (saturated fat 9g) • FIBER 5g • SODIUM 627mg

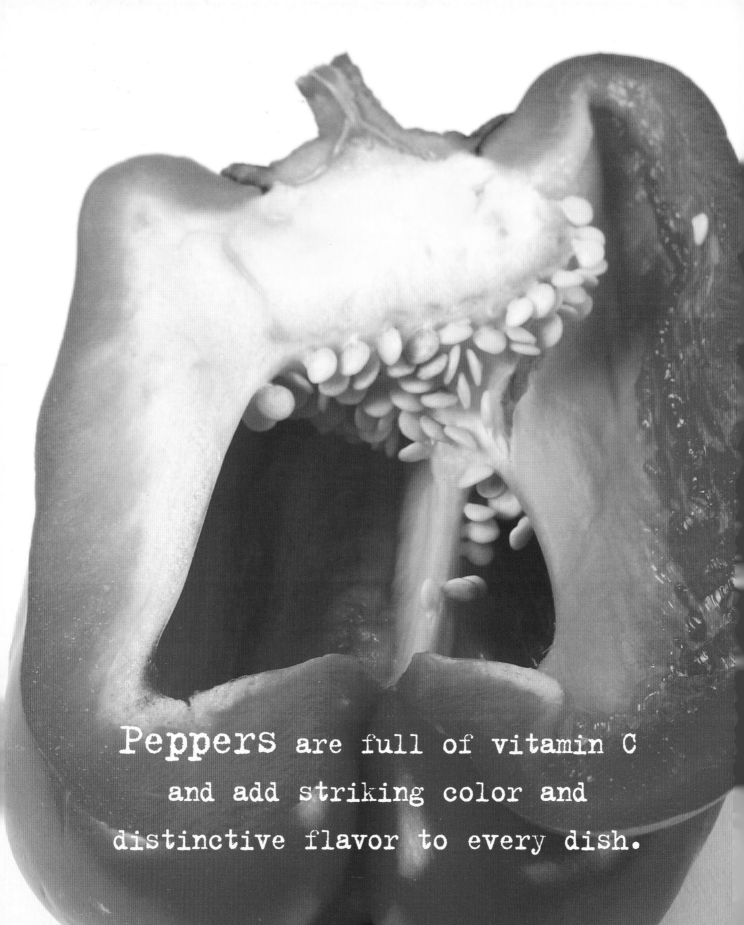

Peppers are full of vitamin C and add striking color and distinctive flavor to every dish.

PEPPERS STUFFED WITH MINTED RICE

Sweet roasted peppers are filled with savory rice and topped with the sharp tang of feta cheese.

4 red bell peppers, cut in half lengthwise, seeds removed but stems left on
3 sun-dried tomatoes in oil, chopped, plus 2 teaspoons of the oil
1 cup (150g) finely chopped onion
1–2 cloves garlic, crushed
1 cup (200g) long-grain white rice
2 cups (450ml) vegetable stock or water
4 tablespoons dry white wine
1 pound (450g) plum tomatoes

6 large green olives, pitted and chopped
2 scallions, finely chopped
3 tablespoons pine nuts, toasted
2–3 tablespoons chopped fresh mint
Salt and black pepper
4 ounces (100g) feta cheese, drained and crumbled

PREPARATION TIME 20–30 minutes
COOKING TIME 50–55 minutes
SERVES 4

1 Preheat the oven to 400°F (200°C). Place the peppers closely together, cut side up, in an ovenproof dish and bake for 20 minutes, or until softened. Remove from the oven and set aside. **2** Meanwhile, heat 2 teaspoons of oil from the jar of sun-dried tomatoes in a large nonstick saucepan and sauté the onions for 5 minutes, or until softened. Add the garlic and sun-dried tomatoes and continue cooking for another 2 minutes, then stir in the rice. **3** Pour the stock and wine into the rice mixture, stir well, and bring to a boil. Cover and simmer for 15–20 minutes, until the liquid has been absorbed and the rice is tender. Add a little more water if the rice dries out during cooking. **4** Meanwhile, cover the tomatoes with boiling water, leave for 1 minute, then skin, seed, and chop them. Add them to the cooked rice mixture with the olives, scallions, pine nuts, and mint; season well and stir to combine. Spoon the rice into the peppers and sprinkle the feta cheese over the top. **5** Return the peppers to the top shelf of the oven and bake for another 15 minutes, then serve.

NUTRIENTS PER SERVING CAL 412 • CARBOHYDRATE 57g (sugars 16g) • PROTEIN 11g • FAT 14g (saturated fat 4g) • FIBER 4g • SODIUM 735mg

ggs and cheese

EGGS AND CHEESE

VEGETARIAN SCOTCH EGGS

Here's a vegetarian version of a popular Scottish specialty, using kidney beans and a delicious mixture of herbs and seeds to make a firm, tasty outer coating. Serve it with a green salad and a mustard sauce made from English mustard and sour cream.

1 tablespoon sunflower oil
1 small onion, finely chopped
1 clove garlic, crushed
2 cups (400g) canned kidney beans, drained and rinsed
3 ounces (85g) aged Cheddar cheese, grated
2 teaspoons finely chopped fresh sage
1 teaspoon sesame seeds
1 teaspoon sunflower seeds

Salt and black pepper
4 small eggs, hard-cooked and peeled, plus 1 large egg for coating
½ cup (55g) dried whole-wheat bread crumbs
Peanut oil for deep-frying

PREPARATION TIME 30 minutes
COOKING TIME 15 minutes
SERVES 4

1 Heat the sunflower oil in the frying pan, add the onion, and sauté for 4–5 minutes until soft. Add the garlic and cook for another minute. **2** Put the kidney beans in a blender or food processor. Add the onion and garlic, cheese, sage, sesame and sunflower seeds, and salt and pepper to taste. Puree until combined. **3** Divide the mixture into four and, using wet hands, mold each portion evenly around an egg. **4** For the coating, crack the raw egg into a small, shallow bowl and beat with a little salt. Put the bread crumbs in a separate bowl. Toss each coated egg in the beaten egg, then in the bread crumbs. Transfer to a plate and chill for 10–15 minutes. **5** In a deep-fat fryer, heat the peanut oil. Deep-fry the eggs, in two batches, for 1–2 minutes, until golden. Drain on paper towels and serve hot or cold.

NUTRIENTS PER SERVING CAL 477 • CARBOHYDRATE 26g (sugars 14g) • PROTEIN 24g • FAT 31g (saturated fat 9g) • FIBER 7g • SODIUM 756mg

CREAMY CURRIED EGGS

A coconut curry sauce goes beautifully with eggs, and an aromatic vegetable pilaf is perfect alongside. This spicy dish is so well balanced nutritionally that it needs no accompaniment.

2 tablespoons unsalted butter
1 small onion, very finely chopped
1 garlic clove, crushed
1 tablespoon curry paste
1 14-ounce (200g) can chopped tomatoes
6 tablespoons coconut milk
2 tablespoons chopped fresh cilantro
8 eggs, room temperature

CAULIFLOWER AND PEA PILAF
1 tablespoon sunflower oil
6 ounces (170g) small cauliflower florets
1 fresh red chile, seeded and very finely chopped
1 cinnamon stick, halved
4 whole cloves
1 bay leaf
1¼ cups (250g) basmati rice
2⅔ cups (600ml) vegetable stock
1 cup (150g) frozen peas
Salt and black pepper

TO GARNISH sprigs of cilantro

TOTAL TIME 45 minutes
SERVES 4

1 Melt the butter in a nonstick saucepan and gently sauté the onion for 7–8 minutes, until softened. Stir in the garlic and curry paste and cook for another minute. Add the chopped tomatoes with their juice and simmer for 10 minutes or until fairly thick. Stir in the coconut milk and simmer for another 5 minutes. Add the cilantro and season with salt and pepper to taste. Cover and keep warm. **2** To make the pilaf, heat the oil in a heavy saucepan, add the cauliflower florets, and cook over medium heat for 1–2 minutes, stirring frequently, until just beginning to color. Stir in the chile, cinnamon stick, cloves, and bay leaf, and cook for another 30 seconds. **3** Add the rice and stir well to mix with the vegetables and spices. Pour in the stock. Bring to a boil, then reduce the heat, cover, and simmer gently for 5 minutes. Stir in the peas, cover the pan again, and cook for another 7–10 minutes, until the rice is tender and all the stock has been absorbed. Season with salt and pepper to taste. **4** While the pilaf is cooking, hard-cook the eggs. Put them into a saucepan and cover with lukewarm water. Bring to a boil, then reduce the heat and simmer for 7 minutes. Remove the eggs with a slotted spoon and place in a bowl of cold water. When they are cool enough to handle, peel off their shells and cut them in half lengthwise. **5** Arrange the egg halves on warmed serving plates and spoon over the coconut sauce. Serve with the pilaf, removing the bay leaf and whole spices first, if preferred. Garnish with sprigs of fresh cilantro.

NUTRIENTS PER SERVING CAL 528 • CARBOHYDRATE 59g (sugars 6g) • PROTEIN 25g • FAT 22g (saturated fat 7g) • FIBER 3g • SODIUM 601mg

Not just delicious and satisfying, whole-grain **bread** also helps to ward off intestinal diseases and lower cholesterol levels.

CHEESE-AND-ONION RAREBIT

Here is a richly flavored rarebit made with mature Cheddar cheese, thickened with bread crumbs to add texture, and spooned over thinly sliced red onions before being broiled until golden and bubbling. A spinach, apple, and celery salad is the perfect partner.

6 tablespoons 2 percent milk
½ teaspoon mustard powder
4 ounces (125g) well-flavored aged Cheddar cheese, grated
1 cup (40g) fresh whole-wheat bread crumbs
4 thick slices whole-wheat bread
1 small red onion, very thinly sliced

BABY SPINACH, APPLE, AND CELERY SALAD
1 tablespoon walnut or hazelnut oil
2 teaspoons red wine vinegar
2 teaspoons poppy seeds
Salt and black pepper
8 ounces (200g) baby spinach leaves
2 apples, quartered, cored, and sliced
2 celery sticks, sliced

PREPARATION TIME 15 minutes, plus 5 minutes standing
COOKING TIME 2–3 minutes
SERVES 4

1 Preheat the broiler. Combine the milk, mustard powder, and cheese in a small heavy saucepan and stir over a gentle heat until the cheese has melted and the mixture is smooth. Remove from the heat and stir in the bread crumbs. Cool for 3–4 minutes, stirring occasionally, until thickened to a spreading consistency. **2** Meanwhile, arrange the slices of bread on a baking sheet and toast on both sides under the broiler. **3** While the bread is toasting, make the salad. Combine the oil, vinegar, and poppy seeds in a salad bowl, and season to taste with salt and pepper. Whisk to mix. Add the spinach, apples, and celery, but do not toss. **4** Top the toast with the slices of red onion, then spoon over the cheese mixture, spreading it out to cover the toast completely. Return to the broiler and cook for 2–3 minutes, until the cheese mixture is golden brown and bubbling. Toss the salad and serve with the rarebits.

NUTRIENTS PER SERVING CAL 354 • CARBOHYDRATE 33g (sugars 10g) • PROTEIN 16g • FAT 19g (saturated fat 8g) • FIBER 5.5g • SODIUM 630mg

BUCKWHEAT CRÊPES STUFFED WITH SPINACH AND RICOTTA

A creamy but light filling transforms these nutty-flavored pancakes, popular in Normandy and Brittany, into a great dish for relaxed entertainment. Serve them with tomatoes and fresh basil.

1⅛ cups (150g) all-purpose flour
¾ cup (100g) buckwheat flour
Salt and black pepper
1 large egg and 1 egg white
Sunflower oil for greasing

FOR THE FILLING
10 ounces (300g) fresh spinach
1 cup (200g) cream cheese or quark, at room temperature
½ cup (100g) low-fat cottage cheese, at room temperature

6 tablespoons ricotta cheese, at room temperature
2–4 tablespoons lemon juice
½ teaspoon grated nutmeg
Salt and black pepper

TO GARNISH paprika

PREPARATION TIME 20 minutes, plus 30 minutes standing
COOKING TIME 25 minutes
MAKES 8 crêpes

1 To make the crêpes, sift the flours and 1 teaspoon of salt together. Whisk the egg and egg white together in a small bowl with 2 cups (450ml) water until well blended, then gradually add the mixture to the flour, whisking well. Set aside for 30 minutes. **2** Rinse the spinach and remove any tough stalks, then put it into a saucepan, with the water still clinging to the leaves. Cover and cook over medium heat for 3–4 minutes until it is wilted, then drain well. **3** When the spinach is cool enough to handle, squeeze out the excess water and chop it finely. Mix the cheeses and spinach together and season with the lemon juice, nutmeg, and salt and pepper to taste. **4** To cook the crêpes, heat a small nonstick frying pan over medium-high heat. Stir the batter and check that it is thin enough to pour: if not, add water, 1 tablespoon at a time. When the pan is hot, wipe it with a paper towel dipped in sunflower oil, then pour in 2–3 tablespoons of the batter and tilt the pan until the batter coats the bottom. Cook the crêpe for 1½ minutes, or until the edges begin to brown and curl up. **5** Loosen the edges gently with a thin spatula, then turn the crêpe over and cook it for another 20–30 seconds. Do not be tempted to flip the crêpe too soon because the batter will stick to the pan, and take care not to overcook it; if the crêpe dries out, it will be difficult to fold over. **6** Cook seven more crêpes in the same way, regreasing the pan when necessary. Either fill and serve each crêpe as you go along or, if you want to serve everyone at once, pile the crêpes up between sheets of paper towels and loosely cover with foil. **7** To serve, spread 2–3 tablespoons of the filling along the center of each hot crêpe, then fold one side over the other. Serve the crêpes sprinkled with paprika.

NUTRIENTS PER SERVING CAL 180 • CARBOHYDRATE 27g (sugars 3g) • PROTEIN 11g
• FAT 3g (saturated fat 1g) • FIBER 1.5g • SODIUM 133mg

ONION, FETA CHEESE, AND MARJORAM PIZZAS

In this simple thin-crust pizza, the sweetness of caramelized onions is balanced by the saltiness of feta cheese. They are delicious with a green salad at a buffet lunch.

FOR THE DOUGH
¾ teaspoon sugar
2 teaspoons active dried yeast
2 cups (250g) white bread flour
Salt and black pepper
2 tablespoons olive oil, plus oil for greasing

FOR THE TOPPING
2 pounds (1kg) onions, peeled and thinly sliced
1 tablespoon sugar
2 tablespoons balsamic vinegar
2 teaspoons dried marjoram
5 ounces (150g) feta cheese, rinsed, dried, and crumbled

**PREPARATION TIME 40–50 minutes, plus
1 hour 30 minutes rising
COOKING TIME 35 minutes
MAKES 2 pizzas, each serving 4**

1 First make the pizza dough. Dissolve the sugar in ¼ cup (75ml) lukewarm water, then sprinkle in the yeast and set aside for 10–15 minutes until it is frothy. **2** Meanwhile, sift the flour and a pinch of salt into a large bowl. Make a well in the center and add the olive oil, the frothy yeast mixture, and ¼ cup (75ml) lukewarm water. Stir with a wooden spoon to form a dough. **3** Turn out the dough onto a lightly floured work surface and knead for 5–10 minutes, until it is smooth and elastic, adding extra flour, 1 tablespoon at a time if necessary, to keep it from sticking. If it is too dry, add extra water, 1 tablespoon at a time. **4** Shape the dough into a ball and grease the cleaned bowl with a little oil. Put the dough into the bowl, roll it around so that it is lightly coated with oil, and loosely cover the bowl with plastic wrap. Leave the dough to rise in a warm place for 1 hour, or until it has doubled in size. **5** Meanwhile, to make the topping, bring a large pan of water to a boil. Add the onions, reduce the heat, and let them simmer for 10 minutes, or until they have softened, then drain well. **6** Put the onions into a large nonstick frying pan with the sugar, balsamic vinegar, and salt to taste. Cook them over medium-high heat, stirring, for 10 minutes, or until the liquid has reduced but not dried out completely. The sugar should have caramelized slightly, and the onions should have a rich flavor. Stir in the marjoram and some black pepper and adjust the seasoning, if necessary. **7** Turn out the risen dough onto a lightly floured surface, punch it down, and knead it for 2–3 minutes. Return it to the bowl, cover it once more, and set aside for 30 minutes for the dough to rise again. **8** Meanwhile, preheat the oven to 475°F (240°C). Lightly grease two baking sheets. **9** Turn out the dough, punch it down, and divide it into two pieces. Shape each piece into a ball, then roll it out into a 10-inch (25cm) circle and place on a baking sheet. Drain off any liquid from the onions, then spread them evenly over each pizza and sprinkle with the feta cheese. **10** Bake for 12 minutes, or until the cheese has melted and the edges of the pizzas are crisp and golden. Serve them straight from the oven.

NUTRIENTS PER SERVING CAL 237 • CARBOHYDRATE 37g (sugars 10g) • PROTEIN 8g • FAT 8g (saturated fat 3g) • FIBER 3g • SODIUM 275mg

PIZZA TART WITH CHERRY TOMATOES

A cheese-flavored pizza dough makes a delicious case for a ricotta-cheese-and-herb filling topped with sweet cherry tomatoes and black olives. Serve with a salad of mixed greens and poppy, pumpkin, and sunflower seeds, toasted to bring out their flavor.

FOR THE DOUGH
1⅓ cups (170g) white bread flour
½ teaspoon salt
½ teaspoon instant dried yeast
6 tablespoons Italian-style premium cheese,
   freshly grated, such as Parmigiano-Reggiano
½ cup (120ml) lukewarm water, plus more as
   needed
2 tablespoons extra virgin olive oil

FOR THE FILLING
⅔ cup (170g) ricotta cheese
2 teaspoons chopped fresh oregano
1 tablespoon chopped fresh parsley
Salt and black pepper
8 ounces (250g) cherry tomatoes, halved
16 black olives, pitted
2 tablespoons balsamic vinegar

1 small sprig of rosemary
1 garlic clove, crushed

FOR THE SALAD
2 ounces (50g) pumpkin seeds
2 ounces (50g) sunflower seeds
2 teaspoons poppy seeds
1 teaspoon soy sauce
2 teaspoons sunflower oil
1 teaspoon walnut oil
1 teaspoon cider vinegar
Salt and black pepper
5 ounces (150g) mixed salad greens, such as
   baby spinach, arugula, and oak leaf lettuce

**PREPARATION TIME 35–40 minutes, plus
   1 hour rising
COOKING TIME 15–20 minutes
SERVES 4**

Tomatoes are a real superfood. Lycopene, the pigment that turns tomatoes red, may help to prevent some forms of cancer.

1 To make the dough, sift the flour and salt into a bowl, and stir in the yeast and grated cheese. Make a well in the center. Add the water and 1 tablespoon of the oil, and mix to form a dough. Add a bit more water, if needed. **2** Turn out onto a lightly floured surface and knead for 10 minutes, or until smooth and elastic. Return the dough to the bowl, cover with plastic wrap, and leave in a warm place to rise for about 1 hour, or until doubled in size. **3** Preheat the oven to 425°F (220°C) and place a baking sheet inside to heat. Punch down the dough, then turn it out onto the floured surface and knead briefly. Roll out to a 15-inch (30cm) round about ¼ inch (5mm) thick. Use to line a lightly oiled, shallow 10-inch (25cm) tart pan with a removable bottom, leaving the edges ragged and slightly hanging over the edge of the pan. **4** Mix the ricotta with the oregano and parsley, and season with salt and pepper to taste. Spread evenly over the dough. Arrange the tomatoes, cut side up, and the olives on top. **5** Gently heat the balsamic vinegar with the remaining tablespoon of olive oil, the rosemary, and garlic in a small pan. Bubble for 1–2 minutes or until it has reduced a little, then drizzle over the tomatoes and olives. **6** Place the tart pan on the preheated baking sheet. Bake for 15–20 minutes, until the crust is crisp and golden brown and the tomatoes are slightly caramelized. **7** Meanwhile, make the salad. In a small nonstick frying pan, toast the pumpkin, sunflower, and poppy seeds over medium heat for 2–3 minutes, turning frequently. Sprinkle over the soy sauce and toss together. The seeds will stick together initially but will separate as the mixture dries. Remove from the heat. **8** Whisk together the sunflower and walnut oils, vinegar, salt, and pepper to taste in a salad bowl. Add the salad greens, sprinkle with the toasted seeds, and toss together. **9** Remove the tart from the pan and cut it into four wedges. Serve hot, with the salad.

NUTRIENTS PER SERVING CAL 490 • CARBOHYDRATE 41g (sugars 4g) • PROTEIN 18g • FAT 30g (saturated fat 7.5g) • FIBER 4g • SODIUM 327mg

LEEK AND CHEDDAR CHEESE TART

This tasty tart with leeks, cheese, and a dash of mustard looks as pretty as a picture. Save time by choosing trimmed, cleaned leeks and using ready-made puff pastry.

7–8 slim leeks, about 2 pounds (950g) in total
Salt and black pepper
9 ounces (250g) fresh, or frozen and
defrosted, puff pastry (1 sheet)
1 tablespoon Dijon mustard
1 medium egg
2 ounces (50g) Cheddar cheese

TOTAL TIME 30 minutes
SERVES 4

1 Preheat the oven to 450°F (230°C). Put a kettle of water on to boil. **2** If necessary, trim the leeks to about 7 inches (18cm) and rinse them. Arrange them in a single layer in a wide saucepan or frying pan, pour on the boiling water from the kettle, add a pinch of salt, return to a boil, reduce the heat, and simmer, covered, for 6–8 minutes. **3** While they are cooking, roll out the puff pastry on a lightly floured surface to a 10-inch (25cm) square, then transfer the pastry square onto a baking sheet. **4** Cut a ½-inch (1cm) strip of pastry from each of the four sides. Dampen the area around the edge of the square with water and trim the pastry strips to fit on top of the dampened edges so that they look like a picture frame; press them lightly into place. **5** Drain the leeks and cool them under cold running water. Drain again, then wrap them in a folded kitchen towel, and press them gently to remove any remaining moisture. **6** Arrange the leeks inside the pastry case and brush them with the mustard. Break the egg into a small bowl and beat it lightly, then brush the border of the tart with the beaten egg. Grate the Cheddar cheese and spread it evenly over the top of the leeks. **7** Bake on the top rack of the oven for 15 minutes, or until the pastry is risen and golden and the cheese has melted and is bubbling. Remove it from the oven and cut it into quarters with a serrated-edged knife. Serve hot or warm.

NUTRIENTS PER SERVING CAL 360 • CARBOHYDRATE 30g (sugars 6g) • PROTEIN 12g • FAT 22g (saturated fat 11g) • FIBER 5g • SODIUM 310mg

SPICED POTATO-AND-LEEK QUICHE

If you love quiche but are tired of the usual fillings, here's a new idea to whet your appetite. A vibrant green layer of peppery arugula is sandwiched between sliced potatoes and leeks in a cheese-flavored custard, and the crisp pastry is speckled with hot chile and fragrant thyme.

SUNFLOWER OIL SHORTCRUST PASTRY
1⅓ cups (170g) all-purpose flour
Salt
2 fresh red chiles, seeded and finely chopped
2 teaspoons chopped fresh thyme
1 large egg
4 tablespoons sunflower oil
1 tablespoon lukewarm water

POTATO-AND-LEEK FILLING
12 ounces (350g) waxy new potatoes, scrubbed
8 ounces (250g) leeks, cut into ½-inch (1cm) slices
2 ounces (55g) Emmental cheese, grated
2 tablespoons snipped fresh chives
Salt and black pepper
2 ounces (55g) arugula, roughly chopped
2 large eggs
¾ cup (150ml) 2 percent milk

PREPARATION TIME 30 minutes, plus 30 minutes resting
COOKING TIME 40–45 minutes
SERVES 4

1 To make the pastry, sift the flour and a pinch of salt into a bowl. Stir in the chiles and thyme, then make a well in the center. Whisk together the egg, oil, and water, and add to the dry ingredients; mix together with a fork to make a dough. **2** Turn out the dough onto a lightly floured surface and knead for a few seconds, until smooth. Put into a bowl, cover with a damp kitchen towel, and leave to rest for about 30 minutes. **3** Meanwhile, make the filling. Cook the potatoes in boiling water for 10–12 minutes, until almost tender. Steam the leeks over the potatoes for 6–7 minutes, or cook them in a separate pan of boiling water for 4–5 minutes, until tender. Drain thoroughly and leave until cool enough to handle. **4** Preheat the oven to 400°F (200°C) and put a baking sheet in to heat. Roll out the pastry dough thinly and use to line an 8-inch (20cm) round fluted pan with a removable bottom. Scatter half the cheese over the pastry. **5** Thickly slice the warm potatoes and toss with the leeks, the remaining cheese, the chives, and salt and pepper to taste. Arrange half of the potato-and-leek mixture in a layer in the pastry. Scatter over the chopped arugula, then spread the rest of the potato-and-leek mixture on top. **6** Lightly beat the eggs together in a pitcher. Heat the milk to just below boiling point, then add to the eggs, whisking gently to mix. **7** Place the pan on the hot baking sheet and carefully pour the warm egg custard into the pastry. Bake for 10 minutes, then reduce the oven temperature to 350°F (180°C). Bake for another 30–35 minutes, until the filling is lightly set. Leave in the pan for 5 minutes before removing. Serve warm.

NUTRIENTS PER SERVING CAL 459 • CARBOHYDRATE 51g (sugars 5g) • PROTEIN 17g • FAT 22g (saturated fat 6g) • FIBER 4g • SODIUM 185mg

The tender spears of lightly boiled or steamed **asparagus** are a delicacy best enjoyed when the seasonal produce is at its freshest.

ASPARAGUS FLAN

Asparagus adds vitamins and body to this creamy, elegant flan; roasting the vegetable enhances its delicate flavor. Serve it warm or cold, with a tomato-and-chive salad to add a color contrast.

6 ounces (175g) fresh asparagus, trimmed
1 tablespoon olive oil
6 scallions, trimmed and cut into 3-inch (7.5cm) lengths
2 large eggs
4 ounces (100g) fresh goat cheese
⅓ cup (70g) cottage cheese
4 tablespoons milk
Salt and black pepper

FOR THE PASTRY
1 egg yolk
½ teaspoon sugar
5 tablespoons cold water, plus more as needed
2 cups (280g) all-purpose flour
½ teaspoon salt
½ cup (115g) butter, cut into small pieces

PREPARATION TIME 35 minutes
COOKING TIME 35 minutes
SERVES 6

1 Preheat the oven to 375°F (190°C). To make the pastry, combine the egg yolk, sugar, and water in a small bowl and beat. Sift the flour and salt into a separate bowl. Rub the butter into the flour until the mixture resembles fine bread crumbs. **2** Make a well in the center of the flour mixture and add the egg yolk mixture. Using the back of a knife, stir until the mixture holds together, adding a little more cold water if necessary. Knead lightly, then roll out the pastry on a floured surface and use to line an 8-inch (20cm) quiche dish. Prick the bottom all over with a fork and refrigerate for about 30 minutes. **3** Bake the pastry for 6–8 minutes, until pale but firm. Remove from the oven and set aside. **4** If the asparagus spears are thick, cut them in half lengthwise. Put in a shallow ovenproof dish and pour over 2 teaspoons oil. Roast in the oven for 10 minutes, turning once, until tender. **5** Heat the remaining teaspoon of oil in a small frying pan, add the scallions and sauté over medium heat until slightly softened. **6** Combine the eggs, goat cheese, cottage cheese, and milk in a bowl and beat. Add salt and pepper to taste. Pour the egg mixture into the quiche dish and arrange the asparagus and scallions on top. Bake for 18–20 minutes, until golden. Serve immediately or allow it to cool and serve cold.

NUTRIENTS PER SERVING CAL 480 • CARBOHYDRATE 38g (sugars 3g) • PROTEIN 12g • FAT 32g (saturated fat 18g) • FIBER 2g • SODIUM 452mg

KIDNEY BEAN AND VEGETABLE GRATIN

Raisins, chiles, and fresh herbs add interesting flavors to a rich, warm casserole of rice, vegetables, and beans, topped with cheese and served with Greek-style yogurt.

3 tablespoons virgin olive oil
1 medium onion
2 medium ribs celery
2 cloves garlic
1 medium red bell pepper
¾ cup (125g) seedless raisins
Pinch of dried oregano
Pinch of dried crushed red peppers
1 teaspoon ground cumin
Salt and black pepper
1 14-ounce (400g) can chopped tomatoes
6 ounces (175g) broccoli
Handful of fresh cilantro
1¾ cups (420g) cooked kidney beans
1⅛ cups (275g) cooked rice
¾ cup (125g) fresh or frozen corn
2½ ounces (70g) Italian-style premium cheese, such as Parmigiano-Reggiano

TO SERVE 1 cup (200g) Greek-style yogurt, or 1 cup (200ml) sour cream, and fresh crusty bread

PREPARATION TIME 30 minutes
SERVES 4

1 Put a kettle of water on to boil. Heat the oil in a large, heavy saucepan over very low heat. **2** Peel and chop the onion, rinse and thinly slice the celery, and peel and crush the garlic. Add them to the oil; sauté gently for 5 minutes. **3** Rinse, seed, and chop the bell pepper and add it to the pan with the raisins, oregano, crushed peppers, and cumin and sauté for 2 minutes. **4** Add salt and pepper, the canned tomatoes, and 5 tablespoons of water. Bring to a boil, reduce the heat, and simmer for 5 minutes. **5** Rinse the broccoli, cut it into florets, put them into a saucepan, and cover with boiling water. Bring back to a boil, cook for 2 minutes, then drain and set aside. **6** Preheat the broiler. Rinse and chop enough cilantro to make 4 tablespoons and set aside. **7** Drain and rinse the kidney beans and add them to the vegetable mixture, with the rice and corn. Return to a boil, lower the heat, and simmer for 2 minutes. Add the broccoli and heat for another minute. **8** Remove the pan from the heat, then stir in the cilantro and grate the cheese over the top. Broil the gratin for 5–6 minutes to melt the cheese. **9** Serve accompanied by yogurt and crusty bread.

NUTRIENTS PER SERVING CAL 625 • CARBOHYDRATE 85g (sugars 36g) • PROTEIN 26g • FAT 22g (saturated fat 8g) • FIBER 10g • SODIUM 629mg

CHEDDAR AND BROCCOLI STRATA

A satisfying savory pudding is made up of layers of bread and vegetables with a cheesy egg custard topping. Served with a quick homemade tomato sauce, it is a tasty and nutritious dish. A leafy salad could be served alongside.

1 tablespoon butter
4 shallots, finely chopped
8 ounces (250g) broccoli, cut into small florets
6 ounces (170g) thin green beans, halved
2 cups (200g) fresh or frozen corn
9 thick slices of white bread, 12–16 ounces (400g) in total, crusts removed and slices cut in half
4 eggs
2⅔ cups (600ml) 2 percent milk
2 tablespoons fresh chives, snipped
2 tablespoons fresh parsley, chopped
3 ounces (85g) aged Cheddar cheese, grated
Salt and black pepper

FOR THE TOMATO SAUCE
1 tablespoon extra virgin olive oil
1 red onion, finely chopped
2 garlic cloves, crushed
2 14-ounce (400g) cans chopped tomatoes with herbs
2 tablespoons tomato puree

PREPARATION TIME 30 minutes, plus
  30 minutes standing
COOKING TIME 1 hour
SERVES 6

1 Melt the butter in a frying pan, add the shallots, and cook gently for about 7 minutes, or until softened. Meanwhile, cook the broccoli and green beans in a saucepan of boiling water for 4 minutes, or until just tender. Drain well, then stir into the shallots together with the corn. Season to taste. **2** Arrange six of the halved bread slices side by side in a lightly greased, deep ovenproof dish. Top with half of the broccoli mixture. Repeat the layers of bread and broccoli mixture, then finish with a layer of bread. **3** Whisk together the eggs, milk, chives, and parsley, and season with salt and pepper. Pour the mixture over the layered bread and vegetables, and sprinkle the cheese on top. Set aside for 30 minutes, to allow the bread to soak up some of the liquid. Preheat the oven to 350°F (180°C). **4** Meanwhile, make the tomato sauce. Heat the oil in a saucepan, add the onion and garlic, and sauté over medium heat for 5 minutes. Stir in the tomatoes with their juice and the tomato puree. Bring to a boil, then reduce the heat, cover, and simmer for 15 minutes. Uncover the pan, increase the heat slightly, and cook for another 5–10 minutes, stirring occasionally, until the sauce has thickened slightly. **5** Bake the pudding for 1 hour, or until set, puffy, and golden brown. Just before the baking time is up, warm the sauce gently. Spoon the strata onto hot serving plates and serve with the tomato sauce.

NUTRIENTS PER SERVING CAL 439 • CARBOHYDRATE 53g (sugars 1g) • PROTEIN 23g
• FAT 17g (saturated fat 7g) • FIBER 5g • SODIUM 1012mg

des

and other sweet things

DESSERTS
AND OTHER SWEET THINGS

BAKED APPLES GLAZED WITH PORT

For easy entertaining, this luscious dessert of richly glazed apples with a prune filling can be prepared in advance and then baked just before serving.

4 large apples, cored
16 ready-to-eat pitted prunes, chopped
1½ tablespoons dark brown sugar
2 cups (450ml) port
Zest of 1 lemon, finely grated
Zest of 1 orange, finely grated
2-inch (5cm) cinnamon stick

2–3 cloves, optional
1 teaspoon confectioners' sugar

TO SERVE low-fat Greek-style yogurt, optional

PREPARATION TIME 20 minutes
COOKING TIME 1 hour, 15 minutes
SERVES 4

1 Preheat the oven to 425°F (220°C). 2 Place one of the apples upright and make deep cuts from the top down through it to within 1 inch (2cm) of the bottom to divide it into eight equal segments. Do the same with the remaining apples, then place them close together in a shallow ovenproof dish. 3 Gently push a quarter of the prunes into the center of each apple—they do not have to go all the way down. Sprinkle the apples with the brown sugar and pour the port over them. Add the lemon and orange zests, cinnamon stick, and cloves, if using, to the dish. 4 Bake, uncovered, for 15 minutes. Reduce the temperature to 350°F (180°C) and bake for another 45–60 minutes, basting the apples with the port every 10–15 minutes, until they have softened but not broken up and the port has reduced to a syrupy consistency. 5 Serve the apples on individual plates with the port sauce spooned over them. Sift a little confectioners' sugar over the top and accompany with yogurt, if you like.

NUTRIENTS PER SERVING CAL 363 • CARBOHYDRATE 60g (sugars 50g) • PROTEIN 2g
• FAT 0g • FIBER 5g • SODIUM 14mg

Dried **figs** have six times the calories of fresh figs, but they are a richer source of fiber and minerals.

BROILED FIGS

A gorgeous dessert featuring plump fresh figs, scented with rosewater and oozing with beautiful pink juices.

1 tablespoon butter at room temperature
8 large fresh figs
1 lemon
A few drops of rosewater, optional

6 tablespoons superfine sugar
6 tablespoons crème fraîche

TOTAL TIME 20 minutes
SERVES 4

1 Preheat the broiler to its highest setting for 10 minutes. Lightly butter a small flameproof dish. **2** Rinse, dry, and remove the stems from the figs, then cut them in half. **3** Squeeze the lemon juice into a small bowl and add the rosewater, if using. Toss the figs in the scented juice, then arrange them, cut side down, in one layer in the buttered dish. Sprinkle the skins liberally with 3 tablespoons of the superfine sugar. **4** Place under the hot broiler and broil for 3–4 minutes. Turn them over, sprinkle the cut sides with the remaining 3 tablespoons superfine sugar, and broil them for another 2–3 minutes. Serve piping hot, bathed in their pink juices, with the crème fraîche.

NUTRIENTS PER SERVING CAL 266 • CARBOHYDRATE 38g (sugars 38g) • PROTEIN 2.5g • FAT 12.5g (saturated fat 8g) • FIBER 2g • SODIUM 33mg

SPICED SEASONAL FRUIT SALAD

Use any soft fruit in season for this slightly piquant medley of flavors, a perfect follow-up to a spicy main course. You can add to the glamour of this dish by using lesser-known exotic fruits.

1 large mango
4 ounces (125g) seedless black grapes, cut in halves
4 ounces (125g) seedless green grapes, cut in halves
4 ounces (125g) peaches, skinned, pitted, and sliced
4 ounces (125g) strawberries, hulled and cut in halves or into quarters, according to size
¼ cup (25g) unsweetened dried coconut

2½ tablespoons superfine sugar
Pinch of cayenne pepper
Pinch of mustard powder
Salt

PREPARATION TIME 20 minutes, plus 1 hour, or chill overnight
SERVES 4

1 Peel the mango, cut away the flesh, and thinly slice it. **2** Put the mango into a large mixing bowl and add the black and green grapes, peaches, and strawberries. **3** Finely grind the coconut in a spice mill or with a pestle and mortar. Add the sugar, cayenne pepper, mustard, and a pinch of salt and mix well. **4** Add the coconut mixture to the fruit, stir well, cover, and place in the refrigerator to chill for at least 1 hour, or overnight, to allow the flavors to blend and mature.

NUTRIENTS PER SERVING CAL 160 • CARBOHYDRATE 31g (sugars 28g) • PROTEIN 2g • FAT 4g (saturated fat 3g) • FIBER 3g • SODIUM 6mg

HOT SPICED PEACHES WITH MASCARPONE

The heat of a fresh red chile brings out the exquisite sweetness of the peaches in this surprising spicy dessert, while sweetened mascarpone cheese makes a refreshing alternative to cream.

⅔ cup (125g) superfine sugar
2 star anise
½-inch (1cm) cinnamon stick
1 fresh red chile
2 thin slices fresh ginger

1 lemon
2 pounds (1kg) firm but ripe peaches
¾ cup (175g) mascarpone cheese

TIME 25 minutes
SERVES 4

1 Put a kettle of water on to boil. Pour ¾ cup (150ml) water into a large saucepan and add ½ cup (115g) of the sugar, the star anise, cinnamon, chile, and the ginger. Stir over medium heat until the sugar has dissolved, then bring to a boil. **2** Wash any wax off the lemon, pare off three thin strips of zest, add them to the sugar syrup, then reduce the heat and simmer. **3** Cut the peaches in halves and remove the pits. Put the peaches into a bowl and cover with boiling water. Leave for 1–2 minutes, then drain and peel off their skins. Cut each half into 4–6 slices and add them to the sugar syrup. **4** Bring the peaches to a boil, then reduce the heat and simmer gently for 5 minutes, or until they are just softened. **5** Meanwhile, stir the remaining sugar into the mascarpone, then squeeze the juice from the lemon. **6** Remove the spiced peaches from the heat, then add the lemon juice. Transfer into individual dishes and serve, warm or cold, with a little syrup and the mascarpone.

NUTRIENTS PER SERVING CAL 403 • CARBOHYDRATE 54g (sugars 54g) • PROTEIN 4g • FAT 21g (saturated fat 13g) • FIBER 4g • SODIUM 30mg

GRILLED FRUIT

What nicer way to end a barbecue than with a skewerful of delicious grilled fruit. The confectioners' sugar coating turns a delicious chewy brown, and you can choose whichever fruits are in season.

Grated zest of ½ lemon and juice of 1 lemon
4 tablespoons Cointreau or brandy
2–3 tablespoons honey or brown sugar
1 tablespoon bitters, such as Angostura, optional
1 pineapple, peeled and cored
8 ounces (250g) strawberries, hulled
2 tablespoons confectioners' sugar

TO DECORATE sifted confectioners' sugar

PREPARATION TIME 15 minutes, plus 1 hour, or overnight, marinating
COOKING TIME 8–10 minutes
SERVES 4

1 In a china or glass bowl, stir together the lemon juice, liqueur, and honey, adding the bitters, if using. **2** Cut the pineapple into 1-inch (2.5cm) cubes and add them to the marinade, then add the strawberries. Stir well, taking care not to break up the fruit. Then cover and refrigerate for at least 1 hour, or overnight. **3** Lift the strawberries and pineapple from the marinade, reserving the liquid, and thread them alternately onto eight skewers. **4** Dust the fruit with 1 tablespoon of confectioners' sugar, then place the skewers on the grill, sugared side down, and grill for 4–5 minutes. Remove from the grill, dust the other side of the fruit with the remaining sugar, and grill again, sugared side down. **5** Divide the skewers among four plates and drizzle the marinade over. To decorate, sift a little confectioners' sugar over each, then serve.

NUTRIENTS PER SERVING CAL 180 • CARBOHYDRATE 37g (sugars 32g) • PROTEIN 1g • FAT 0g • FIBER 2.5g • SODIUM 8mg

Pears hardly ever cause allergies and are full of natural sugars, so they provide safe, instant energy—deliciously.

BAKED ALMOND PEARS

Quartered pears are baked in a glorious fruit syrup and topped with almond-flavored cookies or crisp, browned roasted almonds to add a crunchy texture.

3 tablespoons butter, at room temperature
1 tablespoon superfine sugar
4 large, firm, ripe pears
4 tablespoons white wine or orange juice
¼ cup (85g) apricot jam or 2 tablespoons honey
6 amaretti cookies or 2½ ounces (70g)
  blanched almonds

TO SERVE cream or plain Greek-style yogurt

TOTAL TIME 30 minutes
SERVES 4

1 Preheat the oven to 400°F (200°C). Grease a shallow, round ovenproof dish with half the butter and sprinkle the superfine sugar evenly over the top to coat the butter. **2** Peel the pears and halve them, then cut them lengthwise into slices about 2 inches (1cm) thick. Arrange the slices in a single, overlapping layer in the bottom of the dish. **3** Mix the wine with the apricot jam and pour the mixture over the pears. **4** Crush the cookies with a rolling pin or finely chop the almonds. Sprinkle them over the pears. Dot the remaining 1½ tablespoons butter evenly over the pears. Bake in the oven for 15–20 minutes, until the pears have softened and the cookies or nuts are lightly browned. Serve with cream or yogurt.

NUTRIENTS PER SERVING CAL 300 • CARBOHYDRATE 25g (sugars 25g) • PROTEIN 4g • FAT 20g (saturated fat 7g) • FIBER 4.5g • SODIUM 87mg

CINNAMON PINEAPPLE WITH MALIBU

Pineapple in syrup is enhanced with a coconut-flavored liqueur for a tropical dessert.

1 ounce (25g) glacé cherries, halved, rinsed, and dried
⅓ cup (75ml) Malibu or other coconut-flavored liqueur
2¾ pounds (1.3kg) pineapple
2-inch (5cm) cinnamon stick, halved
2 star anise
⅓ cup (75g) packed dark brown sugar
3 tablespoons seedless raisins

TO GARNISH sprigs of mint

PREPARATION TIME 15–20 minutes, plus 45 minutes cooling and 30 minutes chilling
COOKING TIME 30–40 minutes
SERVES 4

1 Put the glacé cherries into a bowl, pour 2 tablespoons liqueur over them, mix well, and set aside. **2** Slice off both ends of the pineapple. Peel it with a sharp knife and, using a small knife, remove the "eyes." Cut the flesh into quarters lengthwise. Remove the fibrous core from each quarter and cut the flesh into bite-size pieces. **3** To make the syrup, pour 2 cups (450ml) water into a saucepan and bring to a boil. Add the pineapple, cinnamon, star anise, and brown sugar and stir until the brown sugar has dissolved. Return to a boil, reduce the heat, cover, and simmer for 8–10 minutes, until the pineapple is cooked but still firm. **4** Remove the pan from the heat and use a slotted spoon to transfer the pineapple to a bowl, squeezing the chunks to remove excess liquid. **5** Add the raisins to the syrup, return it to the heat, and simmer for 15–20 minutes, until it has reduced by a quarter. Stir in the remaining liqueur and continue simmering for 1 minute. Remove the pan from the heat and discard the cinnamon. **6** Stir the cherries into the syrup, then spoon the mixture over the pineapple. Cool and serve chilled or at room temperature garnished with mint.

NUTRIENTS PER SERVING CAL 293 • CARBOHYDRATE 64g (sugars 64g) • PROTEIN 1.5g • FAT 0g • FIBER 4g • SODIUM 19mg

STRAWBERRY CLOUDS

Crushed strawberries mixed into a yogurt-and-vanilla meringue are a light-as-air treat.

8 ounces (250g) fresh strawberries
⅓ cup (70g) superfine sugar
2 large egg whites
1 cup (250g) Greek-style yogurt, chilled
½ teaspoon vanilla extract

TOTAL TIME 20 minutes
SERVES 4

1 Rinse and dry the strawberries and hull them, reserving 4 whole ones for decoration. Put the hulled strawberries into a bowl, sprinkle with 1 tablespoon of the superfine sugar, and crush them with a fork. **2** In a large, dry mixing bowl, whisk the egg whites until they form a soft peak, then gradually add the remaining superfine sugar, whisking well after each addition, to make a stiff meringue. **3** Add the yogurt and the vanilla to the meringue and gently fold them in with a metal spoon. **4** Fold the mashed strawberries and their juice into the yogurt mixture. Be careful not to mix them in too vigorously or the light, airy texture will be lost. **5** Spoon the meringue into four dessert bowls and decorate with the reserved strawberries. Serve immediately, or chill for 2–3 hours before serving.

NUTRIENTS PER SERVING CAL 165 • CARBOHYDRATE 23g (sugars 23g) • PROTEIN 6g • FAT 6g (saturated fat 3g) • FIBER 0.7g • SODIUM 76mg

Black currants have four times as much vitamin C as an orange. Drink their goodness in a juice or use as a fruity cheesecake topping.

BLACK CURRANT FOOL WITH ALMOND SHORTIES

Popular since the 17th century, fools are best made with tart fruits. Victorian cooks favored gooseberries, but black currants make a beautiful purple-colored dessert.

1 tablespoon all-purpose flour
1 egg yolk
4 tablespoons sugar
1 cup (200ml) 2 percent milk
12 ounces (350g) black or red currants, stems removed
2 cups (450g) Greek-style yogurt

FOR THE ALMOND SHORTIES
⅓ cup (85g) butter, softened, plus extra for greasing

3 tablespoons raw sugar
¼ teaspoon almond extract
1 cup (115g) whole-wheat flour
16 blanched almonds, cut into slivers

PREPARATION TIME 45 minutes, plus 4 hours cooling and chilling
COOKING TIME 15 minutes
SERVES 4

1 Combine the flour and egg yolk in a small bowl with 3 tablespoons of the sugar. Stir in a little milk to make a smooth paste. 2 Heat the remaining milk in a saucepan until almost boiling, then stir it into the paste. Return the mixture to the pan and bring to a boil, stirring continuously. Simmer for 3 minutes, stirring, until thickened and smooth. Pour into a large bowl and cover the surface with plastic wrap. 3 Put the currants, remaining sugar, and 1 tablespoon water into a small saucepan and bring to a boil. Remove from the heat, cool slightly, then puree in a blender or food processor. Pass the mixture through a fine sieve, then stir it into the custard. Cover with plastic wrap and leave to cool. 4 When the currant mixture is cool, fold in the yogurt, then divide among four serving bowls. Chill for at least 3 hours. 5 Meanwhile, to make the almond shorties, preheat the oven to 325°F (160°C) and lightly grease a large baking sheet. 6 Cream the butter with the sugar and almond extract until very soft, then mix in the flour. 7 Divide the dough into 16 balls about the size of prunes. Flatten each into a 1½-inch (4cm) round on the greased baking sheet, placing them slightly apart to allow room to spread. Lightly press a few slivered almonds into the top of each. 8 Bake for 8–10 minutes until browned and firm. Leave on the baking sheet for 2–3 minutes, until firm enough to lift without crumbling. Transfer to a wire rack to cool. Serve the fools with the almond shorties.

NUTRIENTS PER SERVING OF FOOL CAL 284 • CARBOHYDRATE 32g (sugars 29g)
• **PROTEIN 10g** • **FAT 14g** (saturated fat 8g) • **FIBER 3g** • **SODIUM 101mg**

NUTRIENTS PER ALMOND SHORTIE CAL 100 • CARBOHYDRATE 7g (sugars 3g)
• **PROTEIN 2g** • **FAT 7g** (saturated fat 3g) • **FIBER 1g** • **SODIUM 34mg**

RASPBERRIES WITH OATS

Crunchy granola or muesli with raisins and almonds make a substantial partner for soft, sweet raspberries.

12 ounces (350g) raspberries
2 tablespoons superfine sugar
2 cups (500g) plain yogurt
1¾ cups (150g) granola or muesli with honey, raisins, and almonds
1 tablespoon honey

TO DECORATE a little extra honey or granola

TIME 10 minutes
SERVES 4

1 Combine the raspberries and superfine sugar in a bowl, mix, and set aside. **2** In another bowl, mix the yogurt with the granola. Add the honey, stirring it in lightly so the mixture is streaky. **3** Divide two-thirds of the mixture among four wide 1-cup (225ml) glasses. Top with the raspberries, then add the remaining mixture. Drizzle a little honey over the top, or sprinkle with granola. **4** If it is served immediately, this dessert has a crunchy texture, but if you prefer a softer, creamier texture, chill it for 3–4 hours before serving.

NUTRIENTS PER SERVING CAL 318 • CARBOHYDRATE 52g (sugars 37g) • PROTEIN 14g • FAT 7g (saturated fat 3g) • FIBER 5g • SODIUM 121mg

RHUBARB, ORANGE, AND GINGER CRISP

Aromatic ginger and tangy orange liven up this warm, fruity dish with a crisp, oaty topping.

1 large orange
1 pound (450g) rhubarb, sliced into 1-inch
  (2.5cm) pieces
2 teaspoons chopped fresh ginger
1–2 tablespoons superfine sugar

FOR THE TOPPING
1 cup (125g) all-purpose flour

5 tablespoons "light" butter, chilled and diced
2 tablespoons raw sugar
½ cup (50g) old-fashioned rolled oats

PREPARATION TIME 15 minutes
COOKING TIME 40–45 minutes
SERVES 4

1 Preheat the oven to 375°F (190°C). Finely grate 1 teaspoon of orange zest and set it aside. Then peel the orange, removing all the pith, and divide the flesh into segments, cutting any large ones in halves. 2 Place the orange segments in a pie dish and add the rhubarb, ginger, and superfine sugar to taste. Cover the dish with foil and bake for 15 minutes. 3 Meanwhile, prepare the topping. Combine the flour, butter, and raw sugar in a bowl and combine with your fingertips until the mixture resembles bread crumbs, or process them for 10–15 seconds in a food processor. Stir in the oats and the reserved orange zest. 4 Uncover the fruit and sprinkle the topping over them. Return the dish to the oven, uncovered, and bake for 25–30 minutes, until the topping is crisp and golden. 5 Allow the crisp to cool slightly, then serve. If you prefer to make it in advance, it is just as delicious served chilled.

NUTRIENTS PER SERVING CAL 306 • CARBOHYDRATE 52g (sugars 19g) • PROTEIN 7g
• FAT 9g (saturated fat 2g) • FIBER 4g • SODIUM 133mg

MANGO SORBET WITH TROPICAL FRUIT SALAD

A rich mango-and-coconut sorbet complements this delightful combination of exotic fruits.

FOR THE SORBET
⅔ cup (125g) superfine sugar
Juice of ½ lemon
1 16-ounce (500g) can mango pieces in syrup,
   drained
2 tablespoons coconut cream
2 egg whites

FOR THE FRUIT SALAD
1 mango, peeled, seeded, and sliced
1 papaya, peeled, seeded, and diced
2 small bananas, sliced
1 star fruit, tough ribs peeled off, then sliced
1 medium pineapple, peeled, cored, and cut
   into wedges
Juice of 2 limes or 1 large lemon

**TO GARNISH 4 teaspoons shredded or dried
   coconut**

**PREPARATION TIME 20 minutes, plus
   15 minutes cooling and at least
   4½ hours freezing**
COOKING TIME 10 minutes
SERVES 4

1 Combine the superfine sugar and 1 cup (250ml) water in a small saucepan and bring the mixture to a boil, stirring until the sugar has dissolved. Reduce the heat and simmer for 5 minutes to make a syrup. Strain the lemon juice into the syrup, then set it aside for 15 minutes to cool. **2** Puree the syrup, canned mango, and coconut in a food processor or with a handheld mixer to make about 3½ cups (800ml). Pour the mixture into a freezer-proof container, cover, and freeze for 2 hours, or until it is just firm. (Use the fast-freeze setting if your freezer has one.) **3** When the mango mixture is frozen, whisk the egg whites until they form soft peaks. Scrape the mango mixture with a fork to form crystals, then use a whisk to beat in the egg whites, making sure they are well mixed. Return the sorbet to the freezer and freeze for 1 hour 30 minutes. **4** Remove the sorbet from the freezer and whisk it again. Press it down with a spatula and return it to the freezer for another hour, or until it is firm. **5** When the sorbet is almost frozen, prepare the fruit for the salad and put it in a bowl. Add the lime or lemon juice and gently toss the fruit in it, then set the salad aside. **6** Heat a heavy nonstick frying pan and toast the coconut for 30–60 seconds, stirring, until it is lightly browned around the edges. **7** Serve the fruit salad with two scoops of sorbet per person, topped with the coconut. Any remaining sorbet will keep, frozen, for up to 3 months.

NUTRIENTS PER SERVING CAL 367 • CARBOHYDRATE 82g (sugars 78g) • PROTEIN 4g • FAT 5g (saturated fat 3g) • FIBER 4g • SODIUM 45mg

HOT FRUIT SLUMP

Fluffy dumplings in a hot fruit sauce served with cooling ice cream make a melt-in-the-mouth dessert.

2 pounds (1kg) mixed soft fruit, such as blackberries, blueberries, raspberries, and strawberries, defrosted if frozen
1 tablespoon superfine sugar

FOR THE DUMPLINGS
2 cups (250g) self-rising all-purpose flour
Pinch of salt
1 tablespoon superfine sugar
2 tablespoons butter, diced

1 egg, lightly beaten
⅓ cup (75ml) skim milk

TO SERVE 4 tablespoons frozen or plain yogurt

PREPARATION TIME 10 minutes
COOKING TIME 30–35 minutes
SERVES 4

1 Pick over the fruit, rinse it if necessary, and place it, still damp, in a wide, deep frying pan or large saucepan. Add the superfine sugar and stir. Cover the pan and simmer the fruit over low heat for 15 minutes, shaking the pan or stirring frequently to prevent the fruit from sticking. As the fruit slowly simmers, it should "slump," or soften, into a textured sauce. **2** Meanwhile, to make the dumplings, place the flour in a mixing bowl and stir in the salt and sugar. Rub in the butter until the mixture resembles bread crumbs, then quickly stir in the egg and milk to make a dough. Divide the dough in half and shape each half into eight walnut-size dumplings—a total of 16. **3** When the fruit has simmered into a sauce, drop the dumplings into it, spacing them as far apart as possible. Cover and continue simmering for 8 minutes, then turn the dumplings over, cover again, and simmer for another 8 minutes. **4** Serve four dumplings per person with a little sauce, accompanied by a tablespoon of frozen or plain yogurt.

NUTRIENTS PER SERVING CAL 392 • CARBOHYDRATE 73g (sugars 22g) • PROTEIN 11g • FAT 8g (saturated fat 4g) • FIBER 6g • SODIUM 402mg

Apricots need to be completely ripe to be eaten raw. Dried apricots, though high in sugar, are a good alternative.

PUDDING WITH CREAMY ORANGE SAUCE

Apricots and apples are topped with a light sponge with walnuts and almonds for a nutty texture.

1½ cups (200g) ready-to-eat dried apricots, cut into chunks

4 apples, peeled, quartered, cored, and thickly sliced

1 cup (100ml) unsweetened apple juice

2 eggs

¼ cup (50g) superfine sugar, plus extra for dusting

6 tablespoons all-purpose flour

3 ounces (85g) almonds, coarsely ground or very finely chopped

FOR THE ORANGE SAUCE
Grated zest of 1 orange and juice of 3 oranges
2 tablespoons cornstarch
2 tablespoons sugar
8 ounces (280g) low-fat crème fraîche

PREPARATION TIME 20 minutes
COOKING TIME 1 hour
SERVES 6

1 Preheat the oven to 400°F (200°C). Put the apricots and apples in a 5-cup (1.4l) ovenproof dish, 3 inches (7.5cm) deep. Add the apple juice, cover, and bake for 30 minutes. Leave to stand, uncovered, while you prepare the topping. **2** Whisk the eggs with the superfine sugar until very pale, thick, and creamy. Sift in the flour and add the almonds. Using a large metal spoon, fold the flour and nuts into the mixture until incorporated. **3** Pour the mixture over the fruit, spreading it evenly to the edge of the dish. Bake for 30 minutes, until the topping rises and browns. Dust with superfine sugar. **4** Make the orange sauce about 5 minutes before the pudding is cooked. Pour the orange juice into a glass measuring cup and add water to make 1⅓ cups (300ml). **5** In a small saucepan, mix the cornstarch and sugar to a smooth paste with the orange zest and a little of the diluted juice. Gradually stir in the remaining juice. Bring to a boil, stirring continuously, then simmer for 2 minutes, still stirring. Remove from the heat. **6** Stir in the crème fraîche and transfer to a warmed pitcher. Spoon the pudding into bowls and serve with the orange sauce.

NUTRIENTS PER SERVING CAL 360 • CARBOHYDRATE 51g (sugars 39g) • PROTEIN 7g • FAT 15g (saturated fat 5g) • FIBER 4g • SODIUM 56mg

FLUFFY BANANA RICE PUDDINGS

A light milk pudding is sweetened with honey and bananas for a nutritional boost. It is a great alternative to a simple rice pudding.

¾ cup (60g) short-grain rice
2⅓ cups (600ml) 2 percent milk
3 tablespoons honey
1 vanilla pod
2 ripe bananas
Finely grated zest of ½ lemon
2 egg whites

Pinch of freshly grated nutmeg

PREPARATION TIME 10 minutes
COOKING TIME 1 hour 15 minutes–
 1 hour 45 minutes
SERVES 6

1 Combine the rice in a saucepan with the milk, then stir in the honey and add the vanilla pod. Bring gently to a boil, then reduce the heat and cover. Simmer for 1 hour–1 hour 15 minutes, stirring occasionally to prevent it from sticking, until the rice is soft and the mixture has thickened but is still sloppy. 2 Meanwhile, preheat the oven to 400°F (200°C). Remove the vanilla pod from the rice. Peel the bananas and slice them thinly, then fold them into the rice with the lemon zest. 3 In a clean, dry bowl, whisk the egg whites until soft peaks form. Fold them into the rice mixture, then spoon it into six 1-cup (200ml) ramekins, or a 5-cup (1.2l) soufflé dish, and sprinkle with nutmeg. 4 Place the ramekins or dish on a baking sheet and bake individual puddings for 10–12 minutes, or the large pudding for 25–30 minutes, until golden brown and well risen. Serve warm.

NUTRIENTS PER SERVING CAL 141 • CARBOHYDRATE 26g (sugars 17g) • PROTEIN 5g
• FAT 2g (saturated fat 1g) • FIBER 0.5g • SODIUM 65mg

HOT RASPBERRY SOUFFLÉS

Raspberries give these individual desserts a beautiful, soft rose color and a delectable flavor. They must be eaten straight from the oven to capture their deliciously light melt-in-the-mouth texture.

1 tablespoon unsalted butter, at room temperature

⅔ cup (115g) superfine sugar, vanilla flavored or plain

8 ounces (250g) fresh raspberries

1 tablespoon kirsch, optional

4 large egg whites

1 tablespoon confectioners' sugar, for sifting

TO SERVE heavy cream

TOTAL TIME 25 minutes
SERVES 4

1 Before you sit down to your main course, preheat the oven to 375°F (190°C). Grease the insides of four 1-cup (200ml) soufflé dishes, or ovenproof cereal bowls, with the butter, then coat them evenly with some of the superfine sugar, pouring out any surplus, and place on a baking tray. **2** Puree the fresh raspberries by pressing them through a stainless steel or nylon sieve with the back of a spoon. Stir in the kirsch, if using. **3** When you have finished the main course, whisk the egg whites with an electric beater until they are stiff but not dry, then gradually whisk in the remaining superfine sugar. Keep whisking until the mixture becomes shiny. **4** Carefully fold the raspberry puree into the egg whites, then spoon the mixture into the dishes and make a swirl on top of each. Cook in the center of the oven, leaving space above for the soufflés to rise, for 12–14 minutes, or until well risen and lightly set. **5** Remove the soufflés from the oven, sift confectioners' sugar evenly over the top of each, and serve immediately, with cream.

NUTRIENTS PER SERVING CAL 174 • CARBOHYDRATE 37g (sugars 37g) • PROTEIN 4g • FAT 2g (saturated fat 1.5g) • FIBER 1.5g • SODIUM 80mg

INDEX

PICTURE CREDITS